VELAZQUEZ

VELAZQUEZ

by R. A. M. STEVENSON

With a biographical study of the author
by DENYS SUTTON
Text revised and annotated
by THEODORE CROMBIE

G. BELL AND SONS, LTD
LONDON
1962

Printed in Great Britain by
The Camelot Press Ltd., London and Southampton

CONTENTS

LIST OF PLATES

(Between pages 86 and 87)

Permission to reproduce photographs is gratefully acknowledged as follows:
For No. 2 (from the Wellington Museum, Apsley House)
to the Victoria and Albert Museum, Crown Copyright. For
No. 20 to the Palazzo Doria, Rome. For Nos. 8, 13, 18 to
the Trustees, The National Gallery, London. For the
remainder, to the Prado Museum, Madrid.

PREFACE

THE critical part of the text of this book made its first appearance in 1895 in a large-paper edition entitled *The Art of Velazquez*. In 1899, the revised second edition was published as *Velazquez* in the series 'The Great Masters of Painting and Sculpture', with the addition of the biographical material in Chapter II, and a bibliography and catalogue compiled by Dr. G. C. Williamson, the General Editor of the series. This new edition was reprinted several times between 1900 and 1914, and a German translation by Dr. Eberhard Freiherr von Bodenhausen was published in 1904.

With the celebration of the tercentenary of the death of Velazquez still fresh in memory, it is felt that the moment is opportune for the attention of modern readers to be re-directed to this brilliant study of the great Spanish painter. Stevenson's book deserves to be read through as an essay, rather than to be consulted for reference, though it does, in fact, provide an admirably balanced account of Velazquez's life, as well as a descriptive analysis of a number of his principal pictures. Inevitably, however, in the sixty-five years since it was first published, new facts regarding Velazquez have come to light, and there has been a measure of re-assessment, both on documentary and stylistic grounds, of certain aspects of his work. In so far as Stevenson's text—and that is remarkably seldom—requires elucidation or amendment, this has been done as unobtrusively as possible in the form of

brief foot-notes: alterations to the text itself have been
virtually confined to the modernization of the titles,
numbers, and locations of the pictures in the Prado
Museum to which Stevenson constantly refers. In
order, however, to bring the book completely up to date,
a short Appendix has been added, in which Stevenson's
perceptive judgements are fitted into the pattern of
twentieth-century Velazquez scholarship.

The Plates have been re-selected with a view to illustrating almost all the pictures specifically mentioned by
Stevenson (as the author himself explains, his book was
prompted by notes taken on a visit to Madrid, and his
selection of pictures for comment is largely confined to
those in that city). No attempt, therefore, has been made
to try and broaden the basis of his survey by including
reproductions of the many fine Velazquez pictures in other
collections which are not actually discussed.

A select classified bibliography has been added of
standard sources and works on Velazquez, and of those
which, since 1895, deal with the special aspects of Velazquez criticism (i.e. impressionism) on which Stevenson
enlarges. The somewhat tentative list of works which
was added by Dr. Williamson to the 1899 edition has not
been replaced: in this connection, the reader is referred to
the most recent *catalogues raisonnés* cited in the bibliography, such as those of Lafuente Ferrari, Pantorba, and,
especially, the definitive new work *Velazquez's Work and
World*, shortly to be published by Professor J. López-
Rey.

BIOGRAPHICAL STUDY

R. A. M. Stevenson: Art Critic

by Denys Sutton

THE fate of the writer about art who mainly confines his activities to journalism is usually to be forgotten. All that remains of his views, often dashed off in the heat of the moment with one eye on the clock or the post, is, at best, a volume of reprinted articles and, at worst, an album or so with yellowing cuttings, doubtless by no means complete. These are the notices of current exhibitions penned either from personal choice or at an Editor's command and, in both cases, they will probably do no more than represent the writer's summary *ad hoc* impressions.

Few are the critics who are sufficiently gifted or fortunate as to be able to incorporate the essence of their ideas in a volume that can withstand the test of time. This is the case with Robert Allan Mowbray Stevenson, 'Bob' as he was known to some of the keenest intelligences of his day. Although the bulk of his writing was devoted to the contemporary scene, Stevenson does not claim our attention owing to any particularly brilliant defence of the major men or movements of his period (not that he failed to grasp much of their importance) but on account of his insight into the contribution of one painter, and this an Old Master—Velazquez. His firm and perceptive understanding of this painter's significance and the relevance of his work for some of the leading artists during the second half of the last century, constitutes his chief claim to fame.

His assessment of Velazquez was enshrined in the readable volume on this artist, which was first published in 1895. It became a bible for art students in the late nineties, as Frank Rutter pointed out, while for one of Stevenson's younger colleagues, D. S. MacColl, it was 'the most substantial contribution to the theory and defence of painting since John Ruskin's *Modern Painters*'. Even to-day, after so much has been written about Velazquez, there is much in it to justify Sidney Colvin's high claim that 'probably in no other book, English or foreign, is the psychology of artistic vision expounded with so much lucidity and resource, or the nature of the purely pictorial, as distinguished from the literary and historical, appeal of the painter's art set forth in such cogent and attractive words'.

Born in Edinburgh in 1847, Stevenson's background was that of the Scottish middle class and his father, Alan Stevenson, was a distinguished civil engineer, and the builder of Skerryvore Lighthouse. His mother was Margaret Jones. On the paternal side, he was thus a first cousin of Robert Louis Stevenson, who was his junior by three and a half years. The two boys became close friends when they stayed together at Heriot's Row, Edinburgh in the winter of 1857-58. Already at this date, it was Bob, ever whimsical, who apparently kindled the spirit of fantasy which later vivified his cousin's imagination, inventing the two make-believe islands 'Encyclopaedia' and 'Nostingtonia', which may well have partly inspired the idea of *Treasure Island*. He also introduced Robert Louis to the pleasures of colouring the printed scenery and figures used in the toy theatres so favoured in the Victorian nursery and which are immortalized in the latter's famous essay 'A Penny Plain and Twopence Coloured'.

Little is known of R. A. M. Stevenson's early years. He was at school at Windermere. Subsequently, in October 1866, he went up to Sidney Sussex College, Cambridge where in 1871 he took his B.A. degree. (He was to become an M.A. in 1882.) In his university days he combined an interest in painting with sport. He excelled as a gymnast and lightweight athlete and his favourite exercise was canoeing. On coming down from the university, he returned to Edinburgh, living with his widowed mother and two sisters, one of whom later married W. Sydney de Mattos. The possession of a modest private income permitted him to go on with his painting, and he attended the Edinburgh School of Art.

By nature he was no respecter of persons or institutions; he was ever a Bohemian in fact. He formed one of the leaders of the set of young men which included Charles Baxter, J. W. Ferrier and his cousin, and came together as the 'L. J. R. Club' (the initials stand for 'Liberty, Justice and Reverence'); this had its meeting place in a pub in Advocate's Close, 357 High Street, Edinburgh. There they began to 'disregard everything our parents taught us', and socialism, atheism and the abolition of the House of Lords, were amongst the topics debated. The tenor of their discussions shocked Robert Louis's father who, fearing Bob's influence would turn his son into an atheist, extracted a promise from him not to talk about religion.

R. A. M. Stevenson was a lively companion for his cousin and, at this stage, close ties of mutual affection linked them.   In the autobiography he started to write in San Francisco in 1880, Robert Louis Stevenson left a colourful account of the youthful Bob, and a generous one too.   He was, were his words, 'the man likest and most unlike me that I have ever met.   Our likeness was one of tastes and passions, and, for many years at least, it amounted in these particulars to an identity.   He had the most indefatigable, feverish mind I have ever known; he had acquired a smattering of almost every knowledge and art; he would surprise you by his playing, his paint-ing, his writing, his criticism, his knowledge of philo-sophy, and above all, by a sort of vague, disconnected and totally inexplicable erudition.'   In a sense the two cousins must have complemented one another.   If the whimsi-cality of the older man helped to teach the younger one to think independently and opened him out generally, the steeliness and sense of purpose that marked Robert Louis presumably attracted and possibly enlivened the more slothful Bob.   And it was significant that in November 1873 Robert Louis Stevenson should have told his egeria Mrs. Sitwell that he had had a letter from Bob 'which both pained and pleased me.   He cannot get on without me at all, he writes; he finds that I have been the whole world for him; that he only talked to other people in order that he might tell me afterwards about the conversation.'   No less significantly Robert Louis emphasized that Bob would never have said this to him personally: this underlines the fundamental shyness and inability to assert himself which formed, one suspects, so much a part of Bob's character.

For an enterprising art student, Edinburgh's scope was

obviously limited and in 1873, R. A. M. Stevenson set out
for the Continent. His plan was to study at the art
academy at Antwerp, but as he seems to have suffered
from loneliness there, he moved in 1874 to Paris,
which by then had succeeded Rome as the mecca for
the modern-minded art student. He enrolled in the studio
of Carolus-Duran, who as a leading portrait painter of
the *avant garde* and a sympathetic if somewhat egotistic
personality, attracted a number of foreign students,
amongst them J. S. Sargent. Carolus-Duran, whose
teaching Stevenson always gratefully remembered, was
an enthusiastic admirer of Velazquez and the Frenchman's
influence in deepening his appreciation of this painter was
handsomely acknowledged in Stevenson's volume on the
master. He pointed out, however, that although Velazquez's name was for ever on Duran's lips, 'it was not
to induce his students to copy even Velazquez'. Moreover, this teacher told his pupils to look at nature and
Stevenson remembered his often saying: 'When you go
into the fields you will not see a Corot; paint what you
see.'

He got on well with his fellows and obviously enjoyed
the opportunity of showing his paces as a conversation-
alist. He was clearly an amusing companion and W. H.
Mount states that he went in for 'hilarious poems on the
general subject of Carolus, which gained currency at the
time, but unfortunately are lost to us because they were
not of a nature to be put on paper'. Also his was a critical spirit, and the independent side of his nature was
signalled out by the American painter, W. H. Low, who
knew him well at this period; as he remarked in his
A Chronicle of Friendship, 'in an imaginary Republic of Art
and Letters, he would have found a place where the gift

of stimulating sympathetic intelligence would have given him a position among the most useful of citizens'.

Paris was just the place for Stevenson and his carefree, entertaining existence there, accorded well with his temperament, in a way, that of a Chekovian perpetual student. During these happy years—for that they certainly were —he lodged at 81 Boulevard de Montparnasse, which was frequented by a number of other students from Duran's, including Low, and 'living on the principal of his small fortune', he would eat at the Veuve Poncelet and, more grandly, at Lavenue in the rue de Rennes, just opposite the Gare de Montparnasse which boasted an excellent Fleurie and which later became one of the best restaurants in Paris. Yet Stevenson did not forsake his Anglo-Saxon habits, declaring that 'every self-respecting British householder should have a barrel of Bass's ale in his cellar'; his was kept in the kitchen. However, he was no loose-liver and once, after having picked up and taken out a couple of laundresses, he made it clear that his intentions had been strictly honourable.

Stevenson had visited France prior to 1874, and, while still an undergraduate, spent a summer at Fontainebleau where he became friends with Auguste Ortmans, once a pupil of Théodore Rousseau's. Many years later he recalled how this painter had showed him the Corots belonging to the Empress Eugènie, which doubtless included the famous 'Souvenir de Mortefontaine' (1864), now in the Louvre. Ortmans had also taken him to 'see work at Barbizon; he set me to paint in the forest, and I learnt that colour was not necessarily a blazing falsity'. After this introduction, it was only natural, once settled in France, that he should have passed much of his time, painting at Barbizon and elsewhere.

The reputation of the landscape school which flourished at Barbizon was such as to attract artists from all over the world—American, English, German, Hungarian and Scandinavian. During his various stays in this locality in the 1870s, Stevenson came across many artists, amongst them compatriots like William Stott and Peppercorn, on both of whom he subsequently published articles in *The Studio*, the Swede Hill and a number of French painters. One of the most attractive sides of the artistic community that settled there and which turned Siron's hotel into a sort of club, was the atmosphere of good fellowship that generally prevailed and of course the internationalism. Low has evoked the spirit of the place and the happy mood that existed. 'The early morning (he wrote) saw us all astir, and a generous bowl of coffee and a bit of bread under the arbour at the back of the hotel having been disposed of, we separated to our work. Those who went far into the forest took a lunch with them, the others, working on the plain or in the peasants' houses in the village, met again at noon. But it was about sunset that one by one we entered the courtyard, shifted our loads of painting materials from our shoulders to the ground, and placed our freshly-painted studies against the wall of the house. Then would come an hour of mutual criticism of our work, as seated at little round tables, conveniently placed, we absorbed various "estrats" in the guise of vermouth, or strolled from one canvas to another.'

With his brown coat rather the worse for wear, his untidy mop of hair, his pipe and the store of hard-boiled eggs which he always took with him on painting tours, Stevenson fitted into this congenial set, and in these days —enchanted days—little money, or coin, as his set called

B

it, was required for a tolerable existence. Much later, he evoked the attractions of the Seine as a painting ground and the unspoiled nature of the countryside, in two spirited papers contributed to the *Art Journal* (1888): thus writing of Yville, he said: 'We found the banks in a perfectly natural condition untouched by the works of man. In some places grass grew to the edge of the steep shores, and twisted roots and branches hung over the stream. . . . No inn existed there, and so during our stay we slept on our boats. The houses of the village are almost huts and the people very simple. When we first landed, queerly dressed and wearing knives, we found it difficult to get a word out of anybody.'

The reproductions illustrating these articles indicate that his painting was close in spirit to the style of Corot and the Barbizon painters. In the 1870s Hill, the Swedish painter, praised his work for being, as he put it, 'beindure moderne'. Low pointed out that his 'gift as a painter, in so far as he was gifted, was in the direction of colour' but also remarked that he was not assiduous in application; significantly, Henley in his article on Stevenson said that 'this wonderful and delightful creature, though he might have stood for the Ideal Artist, had never an art complete in all his fascinating and unique endowment', and observed that his 'pictures were only suggestions for pictures'. As Henley had a good eye, this was probably a just comment. Stevenson was by no means interested exclusively in landscape painting and in 1880 Henley told Colvin that 'he is bent on the figure and on portraiture'. The 'Self-Portrait' of 1875 (which is reproduced in Low's book), painted when he was suffering from mumps, was in the current realistic manner of Carolus-Duran.

Unfortunately, knowledge of the range and character of his artistic sympathies and tastes at this period is regrettably small. Presumably he took advantage of his opportunities to study in the Louvre and elsewhere. Low, for instance, stated that he was an admirer of Botticelli and Filippo Lippi, of the sixteenth-century Venetians, and of Poussin, Chardin and Prud'hon. More unconventional for his era, perhaps, was his liking for Primaticcio and Rosso; this he had gained from Low who, in turn, had been introduced to their work by J. F. Millet; and he was also attracted by French Renaissance sculpture, especially that of Jean Goujon.

He appreciated Puvis de Chavannes and joined Low in voting Baudry 'a great swell'; yet he also considered that this artist revealed the paucity of his imagination by spending four years copying Michelangelo and Raphael. Naturally Corot and Millet were amongst his heroes. He once had breakfast with Corot while Low introduced him to Millet and he told the American on their way home: 'Do you consider it fair play, in a conversation between gentlemen concerning minor poets, to spring Shakespeare on your opponent?' But what did he make of the Impressionists, and did he by any chance see the first Impressionist exhibitions of the 1870s? And if so, were his views similar to those of another young foreign student in Paris at this time, the American J. Alden Weir who, after visiting the third Impressionist exhibition in 1877, wrote to his parents that he had never in his life seen 'more horrible things'?

At this time, Robert Louis Stevenson often went over to Paris to stay with his cousin and join him on his trips to the environs; one echo of such excursions was the delightful essay on Fontainebleau which the younger man

contributed to the *Magazine of Art* in 1884. With his talk
and his views on Balzac and Flaubert, Bob was then considered the dominant spirit, and, to quote Low again, 'in
our dissonant orchestra the baton of the leader was in the
hands of the elder of the two cousins'. They both formed
part of the group, including Henry Enfield, Frank O'Meara
and Sir Walter Grindlay Simpson, Bart ('Cigarette' of the
Inland Voyage), that went over to Grez in 1876 and stayed
at the Hôtel Chevillon where Robert Louis met his future
wife, Mrs. Bella Osbourne. At first, she was thought to
have fallen for Bob, as well she might—given his wit and
dashing appearance.

The extent to which Robert Louis was influenced by
his cousin can only be hinted at here. Some of his friends
considered that Bob, then and later, had turned him in
the wrong directions; Henley reported that Sidney Colvin,
who did not like Bob and feared him, 'still cherishes (or
I'm very much mistaken) a grudge against him for taking
Lewis out of his influence, and making him a Professor
of drink and the shilling whore. That he's wrong in his
facts is nothing.' Be this as it may, Bob undoubtedly
assisted Robert Louis to liberate himself from conventions; and one may also assume that Bob's wonderful
talk, to which many contemporaries refer, sparked off
certain ideas in his cousin's mind. It seems probable that
Bob supplied some of the ideas for the *New Arabian
Nights*, notably the brilliant conception of the Suicide
Club and, when published in 1882, the book was dedi-
cated to him 'in grateful remembrance of their youth and
their already old affection'. The 'Man who sold Cream
Tarts' in this book, Somerset in *The Dynamiter*, and Prince
Otto are apparently partly modelled on Bob. Moreover,
some of Robert Louis's general ideas on realism and

romance (as ventilated in the *Magazine of Art*, 1883), on the place of style and technique in artistic creation, and on painting and music, may well have been derived from his cousin. This would be more than likely and, at this stage, one should remember, Bob saw himself as a painter, not a writer; and for his part, Bob doubtless picked up much from Robert Louis.

Their opportunities for stimulating exchanges of ideas were numerous; none more propitious than the famous canoeing trip they made on the Sambre, Meuse and Somme in 1876 which Stevenson described so happily in *An Inland Voyage* (1878). Bob had designed a leather canoe of his own 'with a niche for everything' and according to his friends, 'a place for nothing'. This was just the sort of romantic adventure, helped along by Burgundy and tobacco, that appealed to him. 'Arethusa', as Robert Louis called Bob, carried the poetry of Charles d'Orléans while composing English roundels. 'But he was unwisely dressed. He is no precision in attire; but by all accounts, he was never so ill-inspired as on that tramp; having set forth indeed, upon a moment's notice, from the most unfashionable spot in Europe, Barbizon. On his head he wore a smoking-cap of Indian work, the gold lace pitifully frayed and tarnished. A flannel shirt of an agreeable dark hue, which the satirical called black; a light tweed coat made by a good English tailor; ready-made cheap linen trousers and leathern gaiters completed his array. In person, he is exceptionally lean; and his face is not, like those of happier mortals, a certificate.' It was hardly surprising that this 'gentleman gypsy', as Mrs. Stevenson once called him, should have aroused suspicions and that the local police arrested him —as a German spy, though only for a short time.

Few facts are available concerning R. A. M. Stevenson's
life at this point. In June 1879 he was certainly at Cernay
la Ville, situated some 30 km. from Paris, where he met
the Danish painter Krøyer, then on his way to Brittany.
This artist, one of the most gifted of the late nineteenth-
century Danish school, put up at the same inn, which
was frequented by a number of other painters, amongst
them Cormon, Dameron and Pelouse. The two drawings he did of Bob and his cousin are lively and that of
Bob admirably captures his good humour. He may also
appear in the picture which Krøyer painted of an artists'
dinner at Le Cernay. Years later he was to praise his
work when it was shown at the International Society in
London. Doubtless a recollection of his stay at Cernay
prompted Stevenson to point out in the *Velazquez* that
Pelouse, who resided there, 'used to say that the gift of
the naturalist lay in the power of recreating the eye of
childhood'.

Throughout these years, Stevenson evidently lived
partly in France and partly in London. He started to
exhibit at the Royal Academy in 1879 and, with the exception of 1883, continued to do so until 1885: he
also sent in to the Royal Institute. He had a number of
different London addresses at this period: 49 Radnor Street
(1879), 16 St. Leonard's Terrace (1880) and 9 Alpha Place,
Regent's Park (1882). In 1884, he was at Hyères where
he helped to nurse Robert Louis, and he was a frequent
visitor to Bournemouth when his cousin lived there shortly
afterwards.

Unfortunately Stevenson's paintings, although accepted
at the Royal Academy, won him little reward. The writer
of his obituary in the *Pall Mall Gazette* (April 19, 1900)
said that Stevenson 'used himself to allude to his failure

to catch the public eye with half-pathetic irony, and to declare, very much in his cousin's manner, that he was a misunderstood genius, who only wanted an opportunity to excel'. Presumably his marriage to Louisa, the daughter of Theodore Pyrland in 1881 (she bore him a son in 1894) necessitated his looking for some more substantial means of supplementing his income, especially as his habit of living off his capital, noted by Low, must have seriously depleted his resources; Robert Louis Stevenson may have had this period in mind when he wrote: 'I remember very well your attitude to life, this conventional surface of it. You had none of that curiosity for the social stage directions, the trivial *ficelles* of the business; it is simian, but that is how the wild youth of man is captured; you wouldn't imitate, hence you kept free—a wild dog, outside the kennel—and came down near starving for your pains.'

W. E. Henley, the author and journalist, and father-figure to many of the writers of the day, seems to have been largely instrumental in prompting him to take up some more regular and lucrative form of employment than painting. One well imagines that this did not appeal to Bob. However, in 1882, he taught a painting class of undergraduates at Cambridge, which seems to have functioned in connection with Sidney Colvin's work there as Slade Professor of Art. He then turned to art criticism. R. L. Stevenson told Low that he had 'sugared' Bob off into literature: 'of course', he wrote, 'he is yet awkward at the trade; has no facture; is bitterly conscious of it; hates the slavery of writing; hates to give up the time when he should paint; but the one brings in something, the other nix. . . .' He had to be locked up while he wrote his copy and, at first, his pages were 'read and marked'—

with the approval of his critical jailers. In this tutorship,
R. L. Stevenson was joined by Henley who persuaded
Bob to write for the *Magazine of Art* in 1885 and 'a pre-
cious job I had to lead him into harness'. He thus became
a member of that admirable team, which included Cosmo
Monkhouse, Julia Cartwright, J. E. Harrison and Martin
Conway, not to forget Henley himself, which made
this review so lively and informative; it printed, amongst
other papers, Henley's excellent piece on Rodin. More
regular employment was found with the *Saturday Review*.
Although Sidney Colvin maintained (*Dictionary of National
Biography*) that Bob began to write on painting and music
for this journal in 1882, the tone of the articles dealing with
art at this time (which were unsigned) suggest neither his
style nor opinions. According to the obituary of Stevenson in the *Pall Mall Gazette* he joined the review, then
edited by Walter Pollock, in 1885: this even maintained
that 'he was, perhaps, the ablest member of an exceptionally able staff of writers which included Professor Saints-
bury, Mr. Andrew Lang, Mr. David Hannay and Mr.
C. F. Keary'.

Stevenson's touch is surely detectable in the excellent
article on 'Delacroix and Bastien-Lepage' (April 18, 1885)
which reveals a close concern with the technique of painting by describing Delacroix's art in these terms: 'We refer
to his (Delacroix's) extraordinary knowledge of the properties and contrasts of different colours—a branch of learning which has been unaccountably neglected by the great
majority of artists. His shadows are never mere dark
masses possessed of more or less atmospheric quality; his
reflections are never mere reproductions of things neglected; they invariably partake of the nature of the colours
of the objects by which they are thrown, modified by

the surrounding masses. How rarely this is the case in the work of other men may be proved by a cursory visit to any picture gallery.' The direct and easy manner of writing associable with Stevenson is also evident in the review of the exhibition of 'French Pictures in Edinburgh' (May 1, 1886), which treats of Corot and Rousseau—incidentally two of his favourite painters—and of the exhibition at the Royal Society of British Artists in 1887, in which he signalled out for special praise Monet's 'The Coast of Belle-Isle, Brittany', saying 'When the truths he conveys become more familiar to us in art perhaps they will be perceived more readily in nature, and accepted as an important part of vision' (December 3, 1887). Moreover the note '"Ave" Whistler. . . .' in the issue of July 1886, is marked by the fairness so typical of Stevenson.

His decision to become a professional critic induced him to refrain from exhibiting his own pictures; the last time he showed at the Academy, in fact, was in 1885. In the following year he produced his translation of Delaborde's fundamental study *La Gravure*.

Pot-boiling, one imagines, was hardly congenial to an inveterate romancer and individualist like Stevenson; now his life must have seemed rather tame after the freedom of Paris, Barbizon and Grez. One of the old set from Paris, W. H. Low, who met him again in London in 1886, noticed that 'in the earlier days he had worn his heart upon his sleeve, and in the awakening from his speculative dream of life, and in the assumption of everyday responsibilities, the daws had pecked him to such purpose that much of his former buoyancy had given place to a subdued and slightly apprehensive manner.' Moreover, he was naturally idle.

Whether he liked it nor not, his work as a critic soon

won him a considerable and deserved reputation. In 1888 he was elected to the Roscoe Chair of Fine Art at the University College, Liverpool. He was the second occupant of this chair which had been founded in 1885; his predecessor was Martin Conway. Unfortunately, there is no very precise record of his teaching there. It would appear that, at about that time, the lectures in art were attended by a class of thirty students and that Stevenson gave a two-term course in architecture for articled pupils preparing for the qualifying examination of the Royal Institute of British Architects. It would be fascinating to have had some inkling of what he said during this course, especially as the *Pall Mall Gazette* obituary stated that he 'delivered some memorable lectures' in Liverpool. While there he published 'Some Notes on the Autumn Exhibition' (Walker Art Gallery) in the *University College Magazine* in 1890. He maintained his London connections and contributed to the *Art Journal* in 1890.

With his individual taste and strong convictions about art, it was hardly surprising that he caused some stir in Liverpool. In a charming and informative broadcast about Stevenson,[1] Professor Isaacs pointed out that 'The City Fathers on the University Council wanted "no dirty Bohemian" to disturb their artistic complacency, or to advise old ladies who attended his lectures (so the legend persists) to tuck up their skirts, put their heads down and look backwards through their legs at the landscape.' The atmosphere of genteel conformity was too much for Stevenson and in 1892, he resigned his chair of which he was the last incumbent.

He explained to Low the reason for his leaving: 'I thought I might hit it off, said he, when I thought of all

[1] See *The Listener*, Vol. xxxviii (1947), pages 944-5.

that my experience would count for with a class of students really interested, and shut up in a big commercial town, without knowledge of all that I have seen. I knew it would be principally lectures, for nothing like the talks Duran used to give us, prompted by works actually in progress was proposed. But what I found was that, in addition to my definite work in the college, I was expected to wear a high hat and a carnation in my buttonhole, and talk mild gossip about Botticelli, Burne-Jones and Frith—actually Frith—at garden parties and afternoon teas. And then there were a lot of pedagogues—duffers who talked about 'schools', and attributions to this and that master—and queried about dates, and the *cinque-cento*, and that rot—and their wives, who wishes to uplift the working classes by means of art, dear good ladies, of course, but—well, I held out as long as I could and then I simply cut it, for no human being could have stood it any longer.' Poor old Bob, one murmurs; one can see it all; scenes in the manner of Mr. Kingsley Amis, *avant la lettre*. No wonder that Arthur Lemon's historical picture of an ancient Briton, for which Stevenson posed and which was shown at the 1895 Royal Academy under the title 'Hard Pressed', was known among a small circle as 'The Escape from Liverpool'.

Nevertheless, the Liverpool years must have provided him with some sort of an assured income, and at least he was spared the bother of having to put pen to paper. And he could get away. Thus he was in Italy in 1891, though as Henley remarked: 'And on whose coin? . . .' The Liverpool period enlarged his circle of friends, and he became especially close to Professor Walter Raleigh, the literary critic and essayist who described him in a letter to Edmund Gosse as the man 'from whom I learned more (pastors and masters included) than from any single person I ever met'. They kept up the connection and Raleigh's book on *Milton* which appeared in 1900 carried the flattering dedication: 'To R. A. M. Stevenson whose radiant and soaring intelligence enlightened and goaded me during the years of our lost companionship.'

Stevenson's decision to surrender a post with a regular salary, however small, must have required some courage, especially in view of his known improvidence. However, over the years he seems to have received some financial assistance from his cousin who, as a consequence of paternal instructions, made Bob some sort of an allowance; in the late 1880s, £10 a month is spoken of. Not that the friendship between the two men remained unclouded: in August 1890, Robert Louis Stevenson could declare that our relation is too old and close to be destroyed; I have forgiven him too much—and he me—to leave a rupture possible but there it is—the shadow.' Three years later, Robert Louis complained that 'I am beginning to think twice about sending so much of my money to Bob and Katherine. My people are going to be poor enough; and really R and K are the most indifferent and unfriendly people in the world'.

For Stevenson a return to journalism became inevitable. During the last years of his life, he worked as the art critic for the *Pall Mall Gazette* (1893-99). This paper which was then owned by W. W. Astor was edited by H. J. C. Cust in association with Charles Whibley, a close friend of Henley and a member of the Whistler circle, through marriage. Stevenson contributed some two hundred signed contributions to this paper, the majority of which deal with current shows. Thus he reviewed the Paris salons in 1893 and 1896, the two exhibitions of the

International Society of Sculptors, Painters and Gravers in 1898 and 1899, the Royal Academy, and the various exhibitions at the Grafton and Goupil Galleries as well as at Agnew's and Tooth's. From time to time, he contributed to other papers and periodicals, including *The Studio*. He also wrote the letterpress to accompany Joseph Pennell's illustrated volume *The Devils of Notre Dame* (1894) and three books, the *Velazquez* (1895), *Rubens* (1898) and the posthumously published study on *Raeburn* (1900). Towards the end of his life in 1898, he seems to have considered putting in for the post of Curator of the Fitzwilliam Museum, Cambridge in succession to Charles Waldstein. But this was not to be. In any event, he went into a sharp decline and, after a paralytic stroke, died in 1900 at Chiswick where he was then living. He was evidently in poor circumstances as a number of friends took steps to arrange a pension for his widow, and in 1901 she received a £100 a year from the Civil List and £50 from the Royal Bounty.

Stevenson was extremely popular amongst his colleagues in the art and literary world. Henley wrote that he was 'near and dear' to him, and both H. G. Wells and Thomas Hardy liked and admired him; the latter considered him to be more 'solid' than his cousin. He seems to have been a bubbling over, affectionate sort of person: one can see him in one's mind eye wearing his Jaeger suit (the appropriate costume for his time of life, he felt) perambulating the Bond Street galleries or turning up for the Press view at the Royal Academy. He always liked masquerade: Elizabeth Pennell observed in her amusing volume *Nights* (1916) that 'it had always been Bob's way to play the game of life by dressing the part of the moment'. This was the man who in his black flannel shirt had been denied access (and rightly, one must admit) to the Casino at Monte Carlo.

As a young man he was apparently subject to bouts of pessimism—Robert Louis Stevenson once said that, to him, the future was so black as 'almost to ruin his youth'. In later years he showed no signs of a gloomy disposition. He seems to have thoroughly enjoyed the clubbable world of art and letters with a touch of Grub Street, which existed in the late nineteenth century. Doubtless it recalled to him his early years in Paris and the French countryside. He was especially fond of lunching at Solferino's restaurant, very appropriately situated in Rupert Street, which served a Barsac to his taste. He was a visitor to the Thursday evenings given by the Pennells at their rooms in Buckingham Street, off the Strand, which were often attended by Henley and some of his 'boys', fresh from putting the *National Observer* 'to bed'. At the Pennells he would run into Whistler and they recalled on one occasion Bob telling the Master 'how, one summer day in the Long Gallery of the Prado, where "Las Meninas" then hung, an old peasant with faded blue-green clothes came in, sitting down on the green bench in front, and straightaway became part of the picture, so true was its atmosphere'. Stevenson always used his eyes. Elizabeth Pennell who knew him fairly well and met him in Paris in 1893 when he was there with a group of men who went over to 'do' the Salon, including MacColl, Furse, Whibley, Harland and Beardsley, said that 'every visit to a gallery was to him an adventure and every picture a romance, and the best of it for his friends was that he would willingly share the inspiration which he, but nobody else, could find in the most uninspiring canvas, an inspiration to criticism, that is, not to admiration—he never wavered in his allegiance to the "Almighty Swells" of Art'.

Stevenson was an outstanding talker; conversation was his most congenial medium. 'I have heard the best of my time', said Henley in his engaging tribute to his friend in *Views and Reviews* (1902), 'but among them there is but one R. A. M. Stevenson. Nothing like him has ever passed through my hands.' Alas, few records survive of those who excel in this art, but the tribute to his prowess is considerable. Naturally his cousin acknowledged his skill; 'he doubles like the serpent, changes and flashes like the shaken kaleidoscope, transmigrates bodily into the view of others, and so, in the twinkling of an eye and with a heady rapture, turns questions inside out and flings them empty before you on the ground, like a triumphant conjuror'. 'Spring-Heeled Jack', the pseudonym given to him in *Talk and Talkers*, seems most appropriate. His powers also impressed H. G. Wells who used him as a model for Ewart in *Tono Bungay*: but, he remarked in *Experiment in Autobiography* (1934), 'Ewart is not even a caricature of Bob; only Bob's style of talk was grafted on to him. Bob Stevenson, like York Powell, was all on the side of aesthetic concentration and letting the rest go hang. He could not imagine what the Fabians were up to. They were not real in his universe.' Stevenson, incidentally, considered that Wells was 'an awfully nice fellow with the cut of a man of genius—quite real and natural . . .'.

'The talk came', declared another witness, Mrs. Pennell, 'in a steady stream, laughter occasionally in the voice, but no break, no movement, no dramatic action—the sanest doctrine set forth with almost insane ingenuity. . . . And he would tell the most extravagant tales, he would confide

the most paradoxical philosophy, the most topsy-turvy
ethics, with a fantastic seriousness, never approached except
in the Arabian Nights of Prince Florizel. . . .' 'It was',
wrote his friend Sir Walter Raleigh to W. P. Ker, 'the
incomparable charm of R. A. M. Stevenson that his
real life began when his job ended, and you got from
him, at supper, enough to keep Chambers' printing
press hard at work if he cared to use it in that way. So
he escaped the curse of the actor, the preacher, the
writer, the professor and remained a private gentleman.'

Stevenson's position as a critic and the nature of his
views are more fully understood when it is remembered
that his 'moment of vision' came when living in France
in the 1870s. There he discovered the painting of Corot
and the Barbizon school; their attitude to art and nature
coloured and shaped his own and he was especially sympathetic when dealing with painters whose style corresponded to such men. His essay on Corot in the *Art
Journal* of 1889, which is a masterpiece of its kind, illus-
trates his fluency and his keen affection for a fellow, if
much greater, painter. The following two extracts
illustrate his method.

'I think Corot's marvellously clear good sense, his long
course of early carefulness, the slow growth of his style,
and, above all, its sole foundation on nature, prevented
him, when he once attained the expression of his own
ideas, from ever feeling that doubt of his style and that
uneasy wish to turn back and see if nothing has been left
behind. Do not mistake me when I speak of his style as
founded solely on nature. I do not mean that he brought
no art to his work and that he thought of nothing but
truth. I do not mean that through eagerness for the thing

itself he was indifferent to the way a thing was done. It was *not* all the same to him whether he put on his paint thin or thick so that he got the tone right. Nor was he careless what pattern his composition and handling might make on his canvas, provided he had the warrant of nature for all that he did. . . . Corot was quite sincere in his intention to render the open air, and surely no one denies the reality of open-air colours, or that they are as beautiful, subtle and varied as the pigments in a colour box or the stuffs in a draper's shop. So much for Corot's realism; there is also decorative beauty in his art, as I have hinted, consonant with, and, to my mind, inseparable from, his view of the world. One dare not say how much of beauty is, as it were, realism sublimed. Your eye embraces his pictures in their entirety and nothing distracts or worries the attention. A great part of this unity, this harmony, comes from his logical and consistent rendering of atmosphere, the result of his most unusually complete grasp of the field of vision as a whole. Yet we may detect a residuum that is pure style distinguished from observation of nature.' He was no less perceptive in his comments on Théodore Rousseau: in the same essay, he wrote, and it sums up the master admirably, that 'And so Rousseau would often fall back again almost into the Dutch treatment of a tree. He would hunt, with Hobbema, the individual leaf into the deepest and most mysterious haunts of shadow.'

All, or nearly all, he wrote about modern art was under the spell of the French landscapists of the generation of 1830. But this did not mean that he was blind to the merits of their successors, and some idea of the way in which he read the development of contemporary art may be grasped from his paper on 'The Growth of Modern

c

Art' in *The Studio* for 1893. For Stevenson, painting, after the mannerism of the sixteenth-century, had followed three main routes: Poussin and Claude, Rubens, Rembrandt and Hals, and Velazquez and Ribera. The foundation of modern art, in his view, took place in the 1850s and was represented by pictures like Millet's 'Winnower' of 1848 and Courbet's 'The Stonebreakers' (1850) and 'Funeral at Ornans' (1850); the latter, he claimed, was more 'classic' than David's 'Horatii'. The new school, which then came into being, included men like Chaplin, Puvis de Chavannes, Carolus-Duran, Henner, Bonnat, Vollon, Legros, Delaunay, Whistler, Manet and Fortuny; their influence was paramount in the 1860s and 1870s.

However, it was to Manet that 'unquestionably belongs the chief honour of the initiation of the impressionistic quality that characterizes the new schools. Manet is the great modern originator of that mosaic of just open-air tones which finally supplanted lines and object-painting.' He also spoke of the 'style of expression' as represented by, amongst others, Monet, Carrière, Boldini, Bastien-Lepage, Dangan-Bouveret, and Raffaëlli. At this distance of time, it is by no means easy to understand what he meant by this phrase or the reasons which prompted him to place various artists in specific categories and one wishes that he had expanded on such topics. To achieve a fair assessment of the artistic situation during one's lifetime, especially when dealing with current shows, is invariably and always hard, as any practising critic knows, and Stevenson was well aware that 'there are not more than two or three original men at any one time, not two Whistlers or two Monets.' Moreover, in an admirable article on Whistler in the *Pall Mall Gazette* (December 11,

1895), he stressed that 'for thirty years I have been learning how easy it is to admire and to make others admire cheap facile art, and how difficult it is to understand a work of genius and make others see that it is different from the productions of trained talent'.

Professor Isaacs, who has undertaken a detailed and as yet unpublished examination of Stevenson's critical views, has found no extended comment by him on any of the Impressionists. Nevertheless, his affection for these painters was real, and he was one of the first critics in this country to have appreciated their efforts. This is made clear from his article in *The Studio* and his enthusiastic review in the *Pall Mall Gazette* (May 16, 1898) of the first exhibition of the International Society of Sculptors, Painters and Gravers held at the Prince's Skating Rink in 1898 under the presidency of Whistler. The last left no doubt as to his support of modernism, and drawing a relevant comparison with the Royal Academy annual exhibitions, he declared that:

'Hence it happens that a Royal and national institution opens a show which looks like a vast lumber-room, where people of all conditions and tastes, peers and publicans, have stored their pictures and the coloured supplement-pages that adorn their nurseries. On the other hand, a mere handful of artists fix up a shed and organize a real exhibition, well hung, well lit, and neither overcrowded nor hampered by rules that impose a gilded uniformity upon the frame maker, while they leave the painter free to descend to any depth of silly trifling or commercial baseness. The International seems to be organized rather to satisfy artistic opinion than to tickle the fancy of the shilling gaper or to outrun the illustrated papers in their scramble for the penny of the artless but business-minded multitude. . . .'

These were brave words and startling ones to give the public of 1899 and Stevenson went on to write a brilliant assessment of Manet's 'L'Execution de Maximilian' which, as he said, 'is still new, still surprising, still terrible, still irresistible by the fascination of an inspired but logical impressionism. How natural and reasonable is the concentration of this tragedy, how just the weight and accent of every part!—the bronzed soldiers, their dark blue uniforms, white belts, and gleaming sword-bayonets, the long poised rifles, the smoke and flames, the erect, pallid Maximilian, and, wonderfully subordinate to the focus of attention yet quite essential to the composition, the dizzy glimpse of the swimming hillside and the threatening cloud of spectators overhanging the wall. The scene, flashed upon you in an instant, burns itself upon your memory as the great, unforgettable, the only historical picture of impressionism.'

In the same article, he came out in praise of Degas and Monet: 'Of the profound aerial truth of the shadowed "Dancers"' (116) by Degas, there can be as little doubt as of its exquisite drawing and the entertaining individuality of all its figures male and female. My own eye devours with joy the freshness and the succulence of the often copied, always inimitable art of Claude Monet as seen in "Bassin d'Argenteuil". The effect of sunlit air and a full, direct, shadowless illumination pervades everything and is expressed with delicious truth in the tones of green and black boats, white sails, distant trees, and blue sky and bluer reflections.'

He wrote warmly about Monet in his article (*Pall Mall*

Gazette May 10, 1899) on the second exhibition of the International Society held in the following year and his passage on this artist and other Impressionists is worth quoting:

'Claude Monet appears in a latter and more iridescent phase of his art than was shown at the first International Exhibition by his "Bassin d'Argenteuil". There is little arrangement about the present bold, natural, unfaked, almost uncomposed studies of real light, "Landscape" and "Country Road". It seems strange to remember that the gentle, fastidious folk of the New English Art Club went mad at one time over the almost rude naturalism of this great, unaffected prophet of nature. "Landscape" is nothing but a steam of mist illuminated by the light of dawn, yet it is almost unparalleled in its uncompromising sincerity of vision. Other eminent iridescents shown here are Renoir, Sisley, Klügel, C. Pissarro, and Mark Fisher. One of Renoir's rich solid early works, the enchanting "Portrait of a Lady", will certainly find as many admirers as his later "Bathing", a piece of modelling in coloured light, "Le Printemps" by Sisley, bears the date 1872; it is a rolling landscape admirably modelled, broadly handled, steeped in blue air, and complete with the finish of a quiet style based on impressionism. It differs greatly from Sisley's high dazzling iridescent landscape, "La Plaine de Champagne". Indeed, it and three other Pissarros seem, in the matter of vibrating iridescence, to stand about halfway between the two Sisleys and the grand, solemn James Maris, "A Dutch Harbour" with its sublime depth, its mistiness of gold and gloom, and its shimmers of tarnished silver.'

Yet although Stevenson admired Impressionism and the leading masters of the French school, he did not relinquish

his critical position. Thus when writing about Degas's
'The Ironer', when shown at the New English Art Club
in 1898, he could declare that it was 'not a good example
of Degas. Although it contains beautiful passages, such
as the black hair, neck, and the turn of the cheek into
shadow, great parts of it have been scraped out, and more
especially the shadowed face, once probably as exquisite
a bit of painting as the lovely passages of colour and
modelling which now only lead one up to the disappoint-
ment in the mutilated features' (*Pall Mall Gazette*, April
16, 1898). Or, when discussing Pissarro, apropos the exhibition at the Grafton Gallery in 1899, he observed that
'one should note the loss of structural planes in Pissarro's
later spotted style shown here, and should question oneself as to whether he has gained enough to make up
for the loss of the tranquil beauty of those earlier landscapes at the International' (*Pall Mall Gazette*, June 12,
1899).

Stevenson was more reserved about Neo-Impressionism,
and this is the movement to which, I suspect, he referred
when in the *Velazquez* he wrote 'others hold that whatever
else it may do, it [Impressionism] must represent, like an instantaneous photograph, passing movements by blotches
and blurs, and show you strange and really unimpressionistic
attitudes never seen in life, but mechanically revealed by the
camera'. Support for this interpretation is found in his
article on the Société des Artistes Indépendants (*Pall Mall
Gazette*, April 14, 1896), in which he declared that 'Some
painters study the impression all over the field of sight,
noting comparative definition as well as relative colouring; but at the Champ de Mars most experiments are made
in the qualities of illumination. There are painters who
treat the opposition of light and shadow by vast fields of

simple colour in complementary relation; there are others who, in order to secure the vibration of air and light, break up the complementary effect into a dance of small prismatic spots. In many cases the oppositions of colours are flat harmonies bred from meditation on the palette, and not the record of a sensation received direct from nature. The colours form a decorator's arrangement rather than a painter's expression of air, light, and depth. After long looking at an iridescent picture from the right distance, these spots of blue, orange, violet, red, etc., should effervesce and dissolve, leaving the eye conscious of nothing but a sparkling sensation of light. This comes off seldom, because men have not really felt the effect in nature; because they exaggerate its values, and get wrong ingredients, which will not mix; because they have reduced the expression to a dead formula; because their handling makes too conspicuous a pattern, or because they insist on producing iridescence where there is almost none in nature.' This is a shrewd assessment of the minor followers of Neo-Impressionism; on the other hand, when turning to Signac he spoke of this artist and Valton as 'iridescents who conceive of the prismatic spots as the tesserae of a mosaic pattern, thereby expressing the most ethereal of effects with an architectural draughtsman's conventional and formal rigidity'.

Naturally the main part of his writing was concerned with contemporary English art, and he was often forced to concern himself with painters who may not really have interested him but on whom some comment was expected by virtue of his occupation. Thus he was compelled to evaluate the annual offerings of the Royal Academy and the mediocre painters who were shown in the current

exhibitions. Elizabeth Pennell felt that he was over in-
dulgent: 'How often have we laughed', she wrote, 'at his
amiability to a painter of the commonplace who had happened to be his fellow student in Paris, whose work, as
a consequence, his friendly imagination filled with fine
things that to us were conspicuously missing, and whose
name be dragged in into every criticism he wrote, even
into his Monograph on Velazquez, nor could he be
laughed, or argued out of it.' He may well have been
too kind at times as when declaring that J. C. Hook, who
incidentally appealed to Whistler, was 'perhaps the only
Englishman now alive equally unimpeachable by past and
present standards'. To-day, we would also consider that
his assessments of William Stott and J. D. Peppercorn in
The Studio (October 1894, November 1900) were on the
generous side, but the circumstances were extenuating;
both were old friends. On the whole, he went out of
his way to be fair and to try and see what merits he could;
after all, as a practising painter himself, he knew how difficult it was to succeed and he was open-minded towards
the young, praising D. Y. Cameron, J. B. Yeats, and
Wilson Steer.

   Like most critics, he proved at his best when treating
an artist whom he admired and took seriously; then he
could be not only perceptive but shrewd, and a good
example of his balanced approach is provided by his sum-
ming up of Sargent, who had been a fellow student at
Duran's: 'Mr. Sargent's painting is strict painting, as Bach's
fugues are strict music. He deals with nothing symbolical
and with nothing sensational. He relies on nothing which
may suggest to the mind a poetry which is not visible.
The beauty of light playing on the varied surfaces of
things, that is his matter. Form must be expressed as light

expresses it or veiled as light veils it, and colour must be graduated and harmonized on no other system than the natural method of light' (*Art Journal*, 1888). Another excellent evaluation in the *Art Journal* (1898) was of Millais's painting. 'He has given us a few admirable observations, and some superb passages of paint, yet he has made no style, he has perfected no new view of nature, he has exalted to poetry scarce any of the things he has felt with such keenness of sensation.' These remarks accorded with what he told Low when they looked at Millais's picture, 'Speak, Speak' in the Academy of 1895: 'Truly British art, a touching anecdote—poetry for the middle class.'

During his time on the *Pall Mall Gazette*, Stevenson necessarily devoted much space to the exhibitions of the New English Art Club and sound sense distinguished his comments on some of its leading lights. He saw the dangers inherent in the painting of many members of the New English Art Club, the general tendency of whose work, he maintained, 'inclines towards mannerism and *pastiche*', and he argued that 'the beauty of art lies wholly in style and not in the magical use of its resources to convey perceptions of real character and natural poetry. . . . A landscape which is all style is a piece of bric-à-brac on a level with a fine bit of lacquer or other unmeaning but beautiful and artistic ornaments' (*Pall Mall Gazette*, November 14, 1898). He quickly realized the importance of Wilson Steer in the group and his notes on his work combine justice with a shrewd assessment of his weaknesses. His articles, in fact, mainly hinged on an appreciation of Steer. Thus in the *Pall Mall Gazette* for April 14, 1895 he wrote: 'I have seldom seen a large picture by Mr. Steer that I have not wished altered in some particular, though I might not be able to say how. His impressionism has not always appeared natural enough: here the method of suppressing things has seemed more obtrusive than the thing itself; here drawing and modelling of essentials have been queer or inefficient; or here the whole impression has been merely suggested, not rendered complete and finished, as in the work of Velazquez. In fact, the style of Mr. Steer's work has often been inconsistent, and has resulted in a mere suggestion of the way he saw things somewhat deformed by obtrusive splashy handling, or by exaggerated hints of expressiveness. I think Velazquez would have liked "The Looking Glass" (35); it resembles his few sketches for larger pictures, and speaking for myself it possesses their fascinating power of forcing you to look out of the eyes of the painter. I hold it, therefore, to be genuine impressionism, as well as artistic and decorative painting. One may doubt the justness of a touch or two about the girl's elbow, but the definition and nuancing of the whole scene are admirable. The quality of the reflection in the glass is exquisite, and the real girl's figure swims in a delightful, unobtrusively worked wrapping of atmosphere and light. The composition is graceful, original, ingenious, and unlike some of Mr. Steer's eccentric arrangements, acceptable without reflection. The scene looks so naturally brought together that for a moment you enjoy it without thinking how neatly the figure, its foot, its skirt, its head, the frame of the glass, and its contained reflection are packed into the right part of the canvas.'

Once more he devoted much on his article on the New English Art Club to Steer when in 1896 he signalled out his 'Nude', which was 'not to be passed over, if only because its bold strength at once captures the eye. The idea of triumphing by the sole interest of a realistic study of the nude occurred both to Velazquez and Manet. But realism as they felt it, was large and impressionistic, and quite as nobly conceived as the still life of Vollon or Courbet. Mr. Steer's work, while it recalls the "Olympia" of Manet in certain points, is both less imaginative and conventionalized, and also less strikingly true than the Luxembourg picture. "A Nude" is tight, small, and somewhat suggestive of a wooden doll, while the flesh is exaggerated in brightness compared to the brightest whites of the sheets. Still, it is an honest effort at good drawing and modelling; an effort successful enough in places, as for instance, in the legs, especially the upper leg of the model.'

One of the most striking examples of his day-to-day criticism is his demolition of Tonks, in an article (*Pall Mall Gazette*, April 11, 1899), on the New English Art Club of 1899. 'From the point of view of the naturalist, Mr. Tonks can't paint at all; from the point of view of the learned mannerist, stored full of odds and ends of memory, he teems with inventive ingenuity. He thinks in paint, he babbles in brush-work, stringing together scraps and phrases of style, ghostly reminiscences and fevered visions of Watteau, Gainsborough, Fragonard, Conder, Caillebotte, upon a slender something that is rather a distaste for truth than a definite imagination of his own. If we are to see any traces of the possible Tonks beneath all this we see it in the little children's picture, "Christmas Day", and not in the large medley called "A Pastoral Play". The last is one of those designs thrown off without study and wholly from *chic* to amuse other artists, an improvization full of licence that might enliven a lenient after-dinner audience, not a serious picture backed by research

which can create a mood at any time and can endure for
ever. Mr. Tonks rambles over his canvas, dispensing light
or shadow at his caprice or by the momentary state of
his palette, accentuating anything he likes, omitting what
he cannot draw, mutilating his figures, turning them to
caricature, or here and there, as in the lady sitting with
her back to you in the immediate foreground, rendering
them with an amusing gusto that might have supplied
him with an idea for the treatment of the whole
subject. The picture is a sort of sketch-book not done
from nature and jammed together into a frame. Its
general colour passes through every hue and variety
of mildew.'

During his early days in Paris, when a pupil of Carolus-
Duran, Stevenson had grasped the meaning and importance of Velazquez's painting, above all his technical
innovations and achievement. Thus before his thoughts
had turned to criticism he had laid the foundations for the
principles which were to activate his mind. His other
writings were in a way all related to his main theme—the
particular spirit and contribution of Velazquez. And his
book on the artist expressed his views in their definitive
form. The actual period of time he employed to study
Velazquez in the Prado seems to have consisted of no
more than a few days but this was sufficient for a man
with eyes to see and in tune with his subject. Of that
there is no question. Stevenson really did understand
Velazquez and it was, Henley well said, as if having 'got
into the painter's skin, he explains his man's intentions and
expresses his man's results with a sobriety of method, a
justness of tone, a precision of phrase which makes it
literature'. This is very well expressed; Stevenson wrote
from a full heart and as a painter, not an art historian.

Just because he knew how to handle brushes, he could respond so well to the pictorial innovations introduced by his hero. Henley also underlined that the influence of another painter-critic, Fromentin, is detectable in Stevenson's essay. Doubtless this writer's masterly *Les Maîtres d'Autrefois*, which appeared in 1876 while Stevenson was living in Paris, was known to him, and later on it may have helped him to find the style and tone he desired to use in his own writing. 'From Fromentin descends', Professor Isaacs neatly said, 'the mantle of description of picture and process, the definition of values brought into currency from behind the iron curtain of the studios, the term luminarist which he popularized.'

Stevenson was by no means the only person in England to have written about Velazquez; Stirling-Maxwell, Richard Ford and Edwin Stowe were amongst his predecessors. Yet he was really the first writer properly to assess this painter's contribution. Velazquez was a painter particularly accessible to Stevenson's generation: subject and audience were made for one another. The whole tenor of his book is to make relevant Velazquez's lessons in terms of his own generation. From the 1850s onwards, indeed, *Hispagnolisme* had received a fresh impetus, and Manet, Carolus-Duran, Whistler and Sargent were amongst those who had found inspiration in Velazquez. Thus Stevenson could write that 'one cannot help feeling that Manet, the painter of "Le bon Bock" and other magnificently painted heads, must have felt in close sympathy with the handling of the face of "Æsop". Again when one looks at the "Sculptor Montañás", one thinks of Carolus-Duran; of the Whistler of the "Lady Archibald Campbell" when one sees "Moenippus", and of the

Sargent who painted "Mrs. Hammersley" and "El Jaleo",
when one stands before "The Infanta Margarita" and
"The Spinners".'

In his opinion, Velazquez was the first of the impressionists. But for him, and for many of his circle, impressionism did not mean the dissolution of light and the
use of pure colour, as practised by the French school of
that name. It consisted of an attitude to painting in which
every part of a composition was treated in relation to the
whole. Thus he was one of the earliest to grasp that in
his pictures Velazquez coalesced several fields of vision and
also to appreciate the careful contrivance which went to
make each picture. He saw him as a master of unified
vision. In a passage on the master's later works, in which
the unified vision was particularly marked, he observed
that 'Breadth of view was Velazquez's most admirable
possession; by it he made composition, modelling, and
style the slaves of his impressions. This breadth of view
led him in his later pictures to vary his manner of painting according to the sentiment of his impressions, so that
you will find in his work no pattern of brushwork, no
settled degree of intimacy in the modelling, no constantly
equal force of realization in edges and, in short, no fixed
habits or methods of expression.' Later, on the subject of
what he termed the artist's 'apparent artlessness', he said
that it 'surprises one at first, but becomes in the end a
chief charm of the later Velazquez, who was far too great,
too far-seeing, to care for small affectations of manner.
In these pictures nothing seems to interpose between you
and the mind of Velazquez. You seem to be behind his
eye, able to judge and to feel, with all the power and
sensitiveness of that unrivalled organ. In a word, his work
resembles the fine writing in which style is so docile a

servant of matter, that it never draws attention to itself:
you read as you might eat a meal in the Arabian nights,
served by invisible hands.'

Underlying Stevenson's attitude to Velazquez and to
art in general was a firm belief in the 'dignity of technique'. He pointed out that 'technique in painting, then,
must be understood as the method of using any medium
of expression so as to bring out the character of a decorative pattern, or to convey the sentiment with which you
regard some appearance of the external world'. He was
a contemporary of Whistler and his theories were analogous to those of this painter, who owned, incidentally,
a copy of his book on Velazquez. Like him, he was in-
trigued by the connections between music and painting
and his views may well have been derived from the same
sources—Gautier and Baudelaire. One may surely detect
an echo of the Whistlerian doctrine in his observation
that 'when he leaves nature for art, a man leaves
bright boundless space where he has no dominion for
a dark cloistered place where he is master—master of
a medium susceptible of arrangement by harmony, contrast, and gradation; master to make his material speak
in character, follow a vein of sentiment, express a mood
of seeing. But he must learn to obey what, for want
of a better word, one may call the laws of decorative
effect.'

Stevenson's capacity was such that one can only regret
that he did not write more fully on general artistic problems. However, his book on Rubens, though competent,
does not possess the insight which distinguishes the *Velazquez*. On the other hand, in the lively introduction
written to Sir Walter Armstrong's *Raeburn*, he was concerned with a painter whose style corresponded more

closely to his own aspirations. His gift for clear exposition—always an asset for an art critic—was revealed in the distinction made between the English and French manner of painting—the one in which attention was paid to detailed drawing made on bare white canvas as found with the Pre-Raphaelites, the other consisting of 'a general lay in of the broad masses in their main values of colour'. He considered Raeburn as the heir to a painterly manner of colouring, associated with Titian and Velazquez, and consequently as an important forerunner of the modern movement. Such a man, he claimed, 'wants to go straight at his ensemble, and dislikes the calm laying in and building in of foundations which may be unnecessary or even harmful, and are certainly heart-breaking to a poetic and enthusiastic spirit'. He pointed out elsewhere in this essay that 'The methods of work adopted by Raeburn were not unlike those adopted by such men as Carolus-Duran and Manet, who consciously taught themselves to seek for manner in a way of looking at nature. Neither the Frenchman nor the Scot copied or imitated a manner; they merely returned to that broad observation of real light which had produced both the style of Velazquez and the style of Rembrandt.' This was the method of painting with the *premier coup* in which the work 'might take minutes, hours or weeks; but it passed only through one stage, gradually approaching completion by a moulding, a refining, a correcting of the first lay in'.

As an art critic, Stevenson did not write extensively about the European *avant garde* of his time. That this was so was partly due to a lack of opportunity and to his own absence of ambition. Henley correctly observed that 'had there been no wolf at the door there would have been no R. A. M. S.' As he had no real wish to air his views, he did not mind if he wrote or not, and the books on Velazquez and Rubens had to be dragged out of him. Yet his remarks on Degas, Monet and Pissarro, as well as his comments on the New English Art Club, emphasize that he was never hostile to the modern movement, in so far as he wrote about it, although a prior claim on his affection was exerted by those painters—Corot and the Barbizon school—whom he had learnt to love as a young man in Paris. This is very natural and normal.

When his writings are compared with the bulk of the criticism in his own era, their novelty and freshness become apparent. They are marked by a conversational lightness, and, at times, one feels that he has just broken off from talking in order to write the piece demanded of him. The fact that he was not trying to create 'literature' enabled him to avoid the rather blowsy and arch style favoured on occasion by his cousin or Henley. He was concise and direct in his attack upon a subject; he paid proper attention to technique. In his own day, his approach was revolutionary. It consisted of a belief that painting comprised more than the illustration of a story and that its appreciation arose from an awareness of the properties of paint. 'Oil paint', he declared, 'is the least abstract or conventional of the mediums. It is the medium of the luminarist and the man who would render an account of the full aspect of nature. . . . The beauties of real light by themselves supply a subject for poetry to the seeing eye; yet they by no means exclude—they rather favour, with their language of natural mystery—the revelation of the solidly built beauties of form. . . . This poetry of the real only comes when a man of feeling and insight, setting down his experiences of nature,

D

determines to make the most of the things he loves
best. So doing he shows you how interesting, how
beautiful the pattern and nuances of light may be, even
when it falls upon objects that you have learnt to call
ugly.'

Words like those served to cleanse the eyes of his contemporaries and helped them realize the artistic values of
painting, and Freiherr von Bodenhausen, who translated
the *Velazquez* into German, correctly suggested in his pre-
face that Stevenson's role in England had been analogous
to Hildebrandt's in Germany; both were artists as well.
This concentration upon the essence of painting was of
great importance in preparing the way for the new generation—for D. S. MacColl, who wrote in *The Speaker* and
the *Saturday Review* in the 1890s, and later for Roger Fry
and Clive Bell. It was not Stevenson's method to formu-
late his findings and observations in a scientific manner
and to propound a system of aesthetics; nevertheless, he
achieved a real place in the history of criticism. Thus
his emphasis upon Velazquez's ability to fuse different
fields of vision in one composition, which is evident
in the master's later works, anticipates one of the
main theories outlined by Heinrich Wöfflin in his *Principles of Art History* (1915)—namely that multiplicity of
vision occurred with the Baroque and that a distinction can be made between 'das Lineare und das
Malerische'.

From another angle, Stevenson's role was important.
He was exceedingly independent as a critic and as a man;
and of a cut that is rarely to be met with in our days:
more's the pity. His cousin once defined the Bohemian
as someone 'who lives wholly to himself, does what he
wishes and not what is thought proper, buys what he

wants for himself and not what is thought proper, works at what he believes he can do well and not what will bring him in money and fame'. Such a man was Bob Stevenson—that 'exquisite troll of genius', as Edmund Gosse once termed him.

VELAZQUEZ

INTRODUCTION

THE IMPORTANCE OF VELAZQUEZ IN THE HISTORY OF PAINTING

WHEN one speaks of Velazquez, it must be remembered that his influence upon art is still young. His genius slumbered for two hundred years, till the sympathy of one or two great artists broke the spell and showed us the true enchanter of realism, shaping himself from a cloud of misapprehension. The importance and the comparative novelty of the subject may excuse these few notes, taken during a visit to Madrid. For it will be allowed that Italy still draws the mass of picture-lovers. Hundreds of writers, sitting at home, direct the pilgrimages of thousands of travellers amidst the nicest details of Italian galleries. Every day sees some new book or paper on the Raphaelites, Pre-Raphaelites, or Venetians. You enter the Uffizi of Florence or the Academy of Venice with a crowd who look at their books no less than at the pictures. The Prado of Madrid is almost your own; a few students are there, and a stray traveller or two like yourself, but you may wander half a morning and see no other Englishman. The great gallery has not yet been described and criticized in English more than it deserves.[1] Now people like to attach a ready-made sentiment to a picture; they hate to form their own judgement, and to wait till a canvas speaks to them in its own language. The true effect of art is slow. A picture is a quiet companion of your leisure, whose mood you learn to accept without heated controversy; one of those quiet figures, in fact, who sit and smoke opposite you, till you seem to exchange thoughts with them by something like mental transference. If you must rush this intimacy in a public gallery, you should look at a picture as you would at a mesmerizer, with your head empty and all your life in your eyes. But the hurried visitor sins from over-eagerness. He is fluttered by anticipation of the many things to come, and will not abandon himself to what is actually before his eyes. He will not wait; he prefers to bustle up his acquaintance with a canvas by means of the formal introduction of someone whom he regards as an habitué of picture-galleries.

The energy and eloquence of a Ruskin and the sympathetic comprehension of a Whistler or a Carolus-Duran[2] are needed for Madrid. I do not pretend to have settled my own opinions about Velazquez, much less to set myself up as a guide, or to utter a final word upon such a subject. Someone with time and opportunity, I hope, may take my notes into account, in a thorough investigation of Velazquez, from the point of view of modern art. As yet

[1] There is now, of course, a very considerable body of literature and guide-books in English on the Prado and its masterpieces. For the best of these, see the bibliography.

[2] Emile-Auguste Carolus-Duran (1838-1917) was Stevenson's teacher and mentor in Paris, and is referred to constantly throughout this book. He was a well-known portrait painter who, in association with Puvis de Chavannes and Meissonnier, founded the Société Nationale de Beaux Arts in 1898. He was much influenced by Velazquez, whose works he copied in Madrid.

few but painters enjoy Velazquez, or rightly estimate his
true position in the history of art.   Not much is known
about him.   Contempt, not to say oblivion, fell on the
man who preconceived the spirit of our own day.   Amongst
notable prophets of the new and true—Rubens, Rembrandt, Claude—he was the newest, and certainly the
truest, from our point of view; so new and so true, indeed, that two hundred years after he had shown the
mystery of light as God made it, we still hear that Velazquez was a sordid soul who never saw beauty, a mere
master of technique, wholly lacking in imagination.   So
say those whose necks are stiff with looking at Italy and
Raphael.   Delacroix[1] complains of them, in his Letters,
that they see beauty only in lines, and therefore refuse to
believe that others may receive a different kind of impression.   The opinion of these people is not to be contro-
verted by words alone, and, as nature is a hard teacher, a
student may save himself trouble by studying Velazquez
at Madrid.   A man of genius learns from a mere hint, it
is true, and such an one without going farther than Paris
or London may understand how Velazquez saw the world:
a more ordinary eye, however, must take the Spaniard's
greatness half on trust, if he has not seen Madrid.   But
with the best will in the world some eyes really cannot see
the side of nature that Velazquez saw; while others are so
bandaged by Italian prejudice that they may save themselves the trouble of a journey.

[1] See *Correspondance Générale* ed. André Joubin, Vol. II, 1936, p. 388.
'Ce fameux beau que les uns voient dans la ligne serpentine, les autres
dans la ligne droite, ils se sont tous obstiné a ne le voir que dans les lignes.
Je suis a ma fenêtre et je vois le plus beau paysage: l'idée d'une ligne ne me
vient pas à l'esprit.' (Letter to Léon Peisse, July 15, 1894.)

I

HIS SURROUNDINGS IN SPAIN: HIS POSITION AT THE COURT OF PHILIP IV

TRAVELLING in Spain, after all, is not so bad as many would have it. Neither are the trains so slow and so dangerous, nor the food and wine so unpalatable, as they have been reported, while the approach to Madrid must take you through the scenery of Velazquez's pictures. This provides a fitting overture to the long array of his works which awaits you in the Prado. But in itself no country offers a more beautiful landscape than Spain, and none that I have seen provides a more desirable setting for figures, horses, and other picturesque objects. No trivialities encumber the large structural features of this country. As in the fens, so here, a figure dominates. You see it on the dry, stony foregrounds of empty, rolling plains, which are ringed round with sharp, shapely sierras in the broad, blue distance. The landscape is unembarrassed with detail, but the one or two interesting forms with which it is furnished are at once simple and piquant. A clear, delicate atmosphere, penetrated with a flood of light, softens every definition, and fuses every local tint without blotting it, as in our own foggy island. No local hue appears as if gummed like a wafer against the universal grey paper of everything that is not quite close at hand; nor do the masses of objects look like thin, un-modelled side scenes against an obliterated distance. Things of the liveliest tint sink into the coloured whole, owning, by their lit side as by their shadowed, the federating power of real light. Great parts of Spain resemble pictorially the plains and hills of the Maremma more than any other part of Italy. But the view, although as luminous and as coloured as in Italy, is usually less crowded and less excited, except for the active sport of clouds in this stormier region of Spain. Indeed, the country of Velazquez seems the very place in which to study values, in which to discover and to develop impressionism. On the way to Toledo I saw the sierras, just as Velazquez often painted them, of a powerful blue streaked with stretches of snow, and looking out from an agitated sky full of rifted clouds of a dirty white colour. For Spain is by no means always bright and gay, though always atmospheric and profound.

In this country external nature favoured the painter both by landscape and by picturesque figure; but the inner condition of the people scarcely answered the demands of the historian, who makes art flourish only with freedom and public enterprise. Where was the growing commerce, the expanding institutions, or the religious liberty in the shrinking, priest-ridden Spain of the seventeenth century? As Mr. Whistler says, the growth of art is sporadic, and to affect the mind of one man it is not necessary to postulate the conflict of nations and all the mighty epoch-making machinery of history. Genius is concocted by the momentary accidental commerce of a man and woman, and fostered by a voyage, a visit, or communion with a half-dozen of friends. Commercial demand may encourage trade painting, and princely patronage palatial

decoration; but who shall say what encourages genius—
that compound of original seeing, intellectual courage,
and some gift or other of expression?

Is it encouraging to be a portrait painter, to undergo
the interested but ignorant criticism of the sitter, to disregard times and seasons, the disposition of the moment
and the beckonings of the spirit, and to jump at no ob-
stacle that you cannot clear in your habitual stride? Is
it encouraging to live in a sinking country, and be the
painter of a bigoted and fantastically ceremonious court?
Yet, in spite of such poor encouragement, Velazquez became the boldest and most independent of painters. But
is there no qualifying circumstance? May not the picture
of this life be a transparency that changes when you hold
it up to the light? Many old men, reared in the puritanical
and hypocritical Edinburgh of the past, could tell you the
private, reactionary effect of that life of repression and
humbug upon a decent, genuine man. That you may not
think at all, or act for yourself, is to add the very zest of
piracy to experiment in life and originality in thought.
Where public profession is manifestly a lie, and public
manners a formal exaggeration, life becomes a chest with
a false bottom, which opens into a refuge for the kindlier,
wiser, and more ardent among human beings. As much
as Spain, the court, and the priest, asked of man in those
days, so much you may be sure did the courageous individual repay himself in the freedom of private life, and
in the audacity of private thought. It is, perhaps, this
instinct of reaction that causes the word licence to companion the word discipline in any historical account of an
army. Nothing, they say, was more intimate and freer
than the private bearing of those nobles of the *ancien régime*,
who, nevertheless, stood at arms, so to speak, beneath the

eye of the king on any public occasion. Delaunay, I remember, brought out this distinction of manners, when
he played the part of Richelieu in Alexandre Dumas's
'Mademoiselle de Belle Isle'.[1]

To be a king of Spain, to preside at religious executions,
to have a wife whom no man, even to save her life, might
touch on pain of death, was to be a creature sorely in need
of private liberty, and the solace of confidential intercourse. Philip IV seems to have been naturally kind,
genial, and affable, and to have divided his leisure between
the hunting-field and Velazquez's studio. The two, artist
and king, grew old together, with like interests in horses,
dogs, and painting; thawing when alone into that easy
familiarity between master and old servant, freezing instantly in public into the stiff positions that their parts in
life required. Painter to the king when he was scarce
twenty-five years old, Velazquez escaped most of
the dangers and humiliations of professional portrait-
painting, without losing its useful discipline of the
eye, its rigorous test of the ever-present and exacting
model.

Though remote from Italy, from its living jealousies,
and its overwhelming past, Velazquez was able to copy
Italian pictures in the palaces of Spain, while he was permitted by the king's bounty to visit Rome and Venice
as a person of some consequence. The situation favoured
the growth of a genuinely personal way of looking at the
world; and, indeed, no one was more original in his art
than Velazquez, and no one less afraid of dispensing with
traditional receipts for truth and beauty. He sought more
and more to express the essential quality of his own

[1] Louis Arsène Delaunay (1826-1903), a famous romantic actor. Dumas
the elder's 'Mademoiselle de Belle Isle' was first performed in 1839.

eyesight, and he grew less and less dependent on hints derived from other people's practice. What he painted
therefore concerned him less than how he painted. Like
Rembrandt, who never ceased to paint his own portrait,
Velazquez studied one model, from youth to age, with
unalterable patience and an ever-fresh inspiration. He
could look at the king's well-known head with a renewed
interest, as he went deeper into the mystery of eyesight,
and became better informed as to the effects of real light.
His slow transformation of this face, through a hard realism of feature and detail, to the suavity of impressional
beauty, seems comparable to that tireless climb of the
Greek sculptors, through so many stiffly-studied athletes,
to the breadth of Phidias's gods, or the suppleness of the
serene Hermes of Praxiteles. Unrelaxing criticism of
beauty distinguishes the highest order of artist alone; it
comes from that thirst after perfection which kept the
Greeks satisfied, artistic, even enthusiastic, whilst polish-
ing for three hundred years the details and proportions of
what we should call the same stale old style of architecture. Curious about particular subjects, but incapable of
conceiving a general ideal of sight itself, meaner artists
sicken at the apparently ordinary, or the apparently stale;
and must be cockered up with the pride of lofty titles,
and the conceit of novelty of motif, which they mistake
for originality of view. On the other hand, those who
constantly compare their work, not so much with decorative traditions, as with the beauty they see in reality, keep
their senses active, and scent, even in the apparently
commonplace subject, opportunity for the improvement
which makes for perfection.

The details of Velazquez's life, the dates, adventures,
and disputed attributions of his pictures, can all be studied

in the translation of Carl Justi's book.[1] It is perhaps more amusing to take a turn round the Prado before you have read about Velazquez, before you have heard what picture is doubtful, and when each canvas was painted. One is apt to see too readily in a canvas what one has previously learnt in a book. If one has guessed the dates of pictures, and roughly grouped them into periods, upon no other evidence than the style of the work or the testimony of the subject, one really understands the growth of the painter's powers, and needs the historical document merely to correct trifling errors and to elucidate doubtful points. For this reason I passed two or three days in the galleries at Madrid without any book-knowledge of Velazquez, and without any catalogue. For those who have not much time the plan has its drawbacks. Knowing nothing of the painter's life, they may well overlook matters that have given rise to serious question. It will be well, therefore, to mention one or two significant dates and events in the painter's life, upon the authority of Carl Justi.

[1] For details of the various editions of Justi's *Diego Velazquez und sein Jahrhundert*, see the bibliography. First published in 1888, and in English the following year, it is still the classical monograph for Velazquez studies.

II

PERIODS OF HIS LIFE AND WORK

BY 1599, the year Velazquez was born, his native place Seville had reached the height of its fortunes, and was about to decline from its renowned position as 'the capital of all the merchants in the world'. The site was built upon by successive civilizations—Moorish, Gothic, Renaissance; so that Seville was truly both an 'essentially Oriental city' and a 'very Catholic city'. At the end of the sixteenth century, its Catholicism, though paramount, allowed it to be called a 'city of pleasure', the home of poetry and 'Italian culture'—a town whose Alcázar was named 'The School of Love'. The great painter's family was not of Sevillian origin; his grandfather, Diego Rodriguez de Silva, came to Seville from Oporto, the home of the Silva family. His name, Velazquez, the painter took from his mother, who belonged to an old family of Sevillian hidalgos. Juan de Silva made no attempt to thwart his son's inclination towards painting, but about 1612 he placed the boy with Francisco de Herrera (1576-1656), an architect as well as a painter of religious pictures, low-life and still-life. Dissatisfied with the rough temper of this master, Velazquez left him after about a year, and passed into the studio of Francisco Pacheco (1571-1654), where he remained for five years. Pacheco was a careful and severe teacher of drawing as well as a pedant, a scholar, and the author of a work on painting.[1]   From his writings we gather much information concerning Velazquez, his friendships with artists, and his connection with great personages.

Pacheco felt so satisfied with the birth, the industry, the talent of his pupil that he chose him for his son-in-law, and, on April 23, 1618, married him to his daughter, Juana de Miranda.   Thus the goodwill, the friends, the interest of Pacheco were placed henceforth at the service of his son-in-law.   Among these friends were most of those who took any account of art and letters in Seville. An opportunity to use their kind offices soon occurred. Philip III died on March 31, 1621; the young king, Philip IV, dismissed his father's minister, the Duke of Lerma, and gave his confidence to the Count Olivares, a son of the governor of the Alcázar at Seville. Up to 1615 Olivares had lived in Seville as a patron of poets and painters; when he became the new king's favourite, some Sevillian men of letters spoke to him of Pacheco's son-in-law. Velazquez went at once to Madrid, but it was not till his second visit in 1623, and only then after some delay, due to the arrival of Charles, Prince of Wales, and Buckingham, that Olivares managed to get him a sitting for an equestrian portrait of the king.   A bust in armour (Prado, 1183) must have been painted at the same time as the now lost equestrian portrait.[2]   The likeness pleased, and its author, at twenty-four, received his appointment as Court painter to a king of eighteen.   In this position Velazquez

[1] 'Arte de la Pintura: su antiguedad y grandezas', Seville, 1649.

[2] According to Pacheco, the very first portrait Velazquez painted of the King was completed on August 30, 1623.   It is now lost.   The equestrian portrait, also now lost, was finished nearly two years later, on August 23, 1625, when it was acclaimed on public exhibition in the streets of Madrid. The 'Bust in Armour' is believed by some authorities to be a fragment of this portrait, or a study for it, with some later repainting of the sash.

found himself associated with the Court painters, Eugenio Caxés, Carducho, González, and later on, Nardi. They were not well disposed towards a new-comer who speedily won the favour of their royal patrons and sitters.

Philip IV (1605-65) had two brothers—Carlos (1607-32), and the Cardinal Ferdinand (1609-41). Of these Carlos was the stoutest, the most lively, and the least funereal in aspect; Ferdinand, with the long face of a shrewd but human Scottish lawyer, the most capable and the most active in affairs, while in sport he was second only to the king, who deserved his reputation as the best rider in Spain. Year by year the royal brothers enjoyed more and more the days spent in private expeditions to the hunting-grounds about the Escorial, Toledo, and Aranjuez. These were informal parties, attended only by kindred spirits of whatever rank. The woods of El Pardo, much nearer the capital, were chosen for such great state functions as the 'Boar Hunt', by Velazquez, in the National Gallery. The painter often accompanied the sportsmen, and in the course of his life he made many sketches and pictures of hunting scenes and trophies of the chase, which for the most part are missing.

Isabella de Bourbon (1602-44), daughter of Henry IV of France, and first wife of Philip, disliked sitting, and we only know one portrait of her—that on a white horse (Prado, 1179).[1] This picture is not altogether by Velazquez, who only worked on the face, the horse, and the

[1] Since Stevenson wrote, a second full-length portrait of Queen Isabella has gained general acceptance as autograph on documentary and stylistic grounds. This is the so-called 'Huth' portrait, which was revised by Velazquez c. 1631, as X-rays have revealed that it is painted over an earlier likeness of the Queen, of which a copy has been in Copenhagen since 1663. The head of the Prado equestrian Isabella, retouched and adapted by Velazquez in 1634 for the Buen Retiro Palace, is based on that in the Huth portrait.

landscape. Isabella was an able, as well as an amiable woman, but Olivares gave her no chance to influence Philip. The king's temperament subjected him to female influence, and the minister, fearing the counsels of a wise wife, kept him well supplied with mistresses. Philip had three sisters, whom Velazquez painted. Anne of Austria, the eldest, was the wife of Louis XIII of France, and the beloved of Buckingham; Mary, who married Ferdinand of Hungary in 1629, had been much admired by Buckingham at the time of her betrothal to the Prince of Wales in 1623. Margaret, a nun in the order of Barefooted Carmelites, was painted by Rubens during his visit to Philip.

From the beginning, Philip treated Velazquez in the most friendly manner—coming, says Pacheco, to the studio 'almost every day', by those secret passages hung with pictures, which led from the king's rooms to every part of the old Alcázar. The monotony of this life was broken in the autumn of 1628 by the arrival of Rubens (1577-1640), who for nine months was constantly with the king and Velazquez. At his earlier visit to Spain, in 1603, Rubens saw little of Spanish artists, and complained of their idleness, ignorance, and incompetency. According to Pacheco and others, he thought highly of Velazquez, and delighted in his society, while his view of the king appears in a letter to Peiresc:[1] 'He evidently takes quite a special pleasure in painting, and, in my opinion, this prince is endowed with the finest qualities. I already know him from personal intercourse, as I have a room in the palace, so that he almost daily visits me.'

Rubens worked hard during his stay in Spain, painting

[1] Nicolas Claude Fabri de Peiresc (1580-1637), French scientist and patron of scholars, who bought part of the collection of Rubens. The letter is dated Madrid, December 2, 1628. (See R. S. Magurn: *Letters of P. P. Rubens*, 1955, p. 292.)

E

portraits and copying all the king's Titians. Of course
Velazquez saw him at work, as it is on his authority that
Pacheco gives a detailed list of all that Rubens did. Velazquez, moreover, accompanied Rubens to the Escorial,
where they climbed the sierras and sketched bird's-eye
views of the palace.

It was after his nine months' friendship with Rubens,
and, perhaps, owing to the influence of the Flemish painter
upon the king, that Velazquez was permitted to undertake his first Italian voyage in the train of Spinola, the
conqueror of Breda. This great soldier and statesman was
going out as governor of Milan and commander-in-chief
in Italy. The expedition left Barcelona on August 10,
1629. From Milan, Velazquez went to Venice, where,
according to Palomino, painter to Philip V, he chiefly
enjoyed the works of Titian, Tintoretto, and Paul Veronese. We know, from other sources, that Velazquez preferred Tintoretto before any painter; indeed, we might
guess this taste from his own pictures, even if we had not
the criticisms of Francisco de los Santos on Tintoretto's
work in the Escorial—criticisms which were inspired by
Velazquez, if not entirely borrowed from the *Memoria* or
catalogue drawn up by Philip's painter when he arranged
the gallery.[1] Velazquez avoided Florence, and went
straight to Rome; he copied for some time in the Vatican,
and he spent two months at the Villa Medici, which he
was obliged to leave on account of a tertian ague. From
Rome he passed on to Naples, where he saw, and apparently liked, his countryman, Ribera. In the early part of
1631 he returned to Spain, bringing with him a portrait

---

[1] Padre Francisco de los Santos: *Descripción breve del Monasterio de S.
Lorenzo el Real del Escorial*, 1657. The *Memoria* by Velazquez here referred
to, is now generally regarded as apocryphal.

of the king's sister, Mary of Hungary, which he had painted in Naples, also two figure-subjects, 'The Forge of Vulcan' and 'Joseph's Coat'.[1]

This journey to Italy ends the first part of the painter's life. The long second period, which began on his return, was closed by another visit to Italy in the year 1649. Justi says that the first half of this period was 'probably the happiest experienced both by Philip and Velazquez'. Still, it is true that in 1632 Don Carlos died, and Philip lost his younger brother, the Cardinal Ferdinand, who left Spain to undertake the government of Flanders. Here the cardinal acted with his usual activity as his brother's agent, not only in politics but in picture-buying. He made use of Rubens and his pupils to paint or to procure the numerous canvases which Philip required. The new palace, Buen Retiro, on the heights above the Prado, had been presented to the king by Olivares. This must be decorated, and, later on, the Escorial and the Torre de la Parada—a hunting-lodge in the woods near El Pardo. To this work the Court painters now set themselves, with Velazquez at their head. For this end he produced his 'Surrender of Breda', and his large equestrian portraits; and for this end Caxés, following the lead of Velazquez, painted 'The Repulse of the English at Cadiz' (Prado, 656). Velazquez was now the unquestioned head of the Spanish painters. He had already beaten them all in a competition on the subject of 'The Expulsion of the Moriscoes by Philip III'.[2]

[1] Now respectively in the Prado and the Escorial.
[2] The 'Repulse of the English at Cadiz', one of the series of 'victories' commissioned in 1634 for the Salón de Reinos of the Buen Retiro Palace, is now known, on documentary evidence, to have been painted by Francisco Zurbarán. The contributions of Eugenio Caxés to the series are lost. Velazquez's 'Expulsion of the Moriscoes', described in detail by Palomino, was destroyed in the Alcázar fire of 1734.

The painter was now introduced to a new sitter, the king's little son, Balthasar-Carlos, who was born in 1629, the same year as the illegitimate Don Juan of Austria. In 1638 the Royal Family was further increased by the birth of a daughter, Maria Teresa. Then troubles came thicker upon the Court. After a career of mismanagement, Olivares was disgraced in 1643, and the Queen Isabella, who had regained her influence over the king, died in 1644. In 1643 those invincible lances of Spain, which figure in 'The surrender of Breda', were utterly crumpled up by the great Condé at Rocroi. After the fall of Olivares, Philip exerted himself and went in person to the perpetual war which the French fomented in Catalonia. In 1644 Velazquez accompanied him, and executed, at Fraga, on the borders of Aragon and Catalonia, the most coloured of his portraits of the king. Opinions differ as to whether the Dulwich picture may be the original or a copy of this work.[1] The heaviest blow of all now fell upon Philip; his promising son, Balthasar, caught a cold at Saragossa, and died in 1646.

During this middle period, various people of note visited Madrid, and were painted by Velazquez; amongst others, in 1638, Madame de Chevreuse, first the friend and then the enemy of Anne of Austria.[2] Her visit was immediately followed by that of the Duke of Modena, a great hunter, much beloved by Philip. But the favours

[1] The original of the so-called 'Fraga' portrait of Philip IV is that in the Frick Collection, New York, which was identified by Beruete in 1910 at the time of its sale by the Bourbon-Parma family. The Dulwich version is now considered to be a copy by Mazo.

[2] Marie de Rohan-Montbazon, Duchesse de Chevreuse (1600-79), famous French beauty and opponent of Richelieu, visited Madrid for a few months in 1637-38, as a political exile. She was warmly received at Court, and according to contemporary Jesuit records, was painted by Velazquez 'in the French costume and manner', but the portrait is now lost.

of a friend and a sovereign whose power was declining could not long keep the astute Duke from a French alliance.

During 1634 Velazquez married his daughter Francisca to his pupil, J. B. del Mazo. About 1641-42, his still more illustrious pupil, Murillo (1618-82), came from Seville, and spent two years under the guidance of the master, who completely altered his views, and turned him for a time to the serious study of nature.[1]   Velazquez also renewed his friendship with certain fellow-artists who were employed by the king about this time.   Alonso Cano, Herrera, Zurbarán, the sculptor, Martínez Montañés, his old Sevillian friends, were probably called to the capital on the suggestion of the Court painter.   Velazquez painted Montañés in 1636; Cano, probably, before his conviction for the supposed murder of his wife; and the satirist, Quevedo, certainly before his imprisonment in 1639.[2]

Velazquez left Malaga for Italy on January 2, 1649, landed at Genoa, pushed rapidly through Milan, only stopping to look again at Leonardo's 'Last Supper', and made for Venice, to buy pictures for Philip.   At Venice he made the acquaintance of the poet, Boschini,[3] who tells

[1] Murillo was never a 'pupil' of Velazquez in the accepted sense of the term, though he is said to have been greatly helped and advised by the latter during his stay in Madrid.   The exact dates of this visit (according to Palomino in the early 1640s) are still, however, uncertain, as Murillo is recorded as saying in 1645 that he had never left Seville.   It is more probable that he was in Madrid about 1648-50, when his activities in Seville are not documented, and when the change in his style is consistent with his having studied the works of Rubens, Velazquez and others in the Royal Collections.

[2] The theory formerly advanced that the portrait of Montañés in reality represents Alonso Cano in old age, is not now generally accepted: no other Velazquez portrait is definitely identifiable as Cano.   The prototype of the portraits of Quevedo, like that of Cardinal Borja, appears to be lost.

[3] Mario Boschini (1613-78), poet, painter and art historian.   His *Carta del Navegar Pitoresco*, published in 1660, praises Velazquez.   The Tintoretto study for the 'Paradise' in the Ducal Palace, Venice, is now in the Prado (No. 398).

us that, although not very lucky in his search for pictures,
Velazquez, to his delight, secured a finished sketch by
Tintoretto for the great picture still in the Ducal Palace.
At Naples, Velazquez revisited Ribera, whom he found
much affected by the elopement of his daughter with Don
Juan of Austria, who had seduced her when he was sent
by Philip to quell the revolt of Masaniello. In Rome,
Velazquez met many artists of note, Salvator Rosa, Ber-
nini, Algardi, Nicolas Poussin, amongst the number. He
had the honour of painting Innocent X in his robes, a
task which he did not undertake till he had practised on
a portrait of his studio-fag—the Moor Juan de Pareja—
himself a painter. These two portraits may be said to
stand between the second and third manners.[1]

In the summer of 1651 Velazquez was again at Madrid.
He became more than ever necessary to the king, and
honours fell thick upon him during this final period of
his life and art. He was made Marshal of the Palace, an
office of considerable honour, and, at times, of no little
trouble. He had to arrange the royal journeys, Court
festivities, and tournaments. As Philip, in 1649, had married a second wife—his own niece, Mariana of Austria,
a girl of fourteen—the Court was more lively than when
Velazquez left it, and he had a good deal to do with painting, festivity, and the arrangement and decoration of the
various palaces. By his second wife, Philip had the Princess
Margaret, born 1651, the centre figure of 'Las Meninas';
Philip Prosper (1657-60); Ferdinand Thomas (1658-60); and
his successor, Carlos II (1661-1700), the last of the house.

In 1659 Cardinal Mazarin brought about a marriage

[1] The famous portrait of Innocent X is in the Palazzo Doria, Rome, and
that of Juan de Pareja in the Earl of Radnor's collection, Longford Castle,
Wilts.

between Maria Teresa and his young master, Louis XIV
of France. The marriage took place on June 7, the two
Courts meeting at the Isle of Pheasants, in the river which
marks the frontier between France and Spain. The tedious
journey, the imposing ceremonies, threw a great deal of
work on the shoulders of the Court Marshal, and, a few
weeks after his return to the capital, Velazquez died, on
August 6, 1660.

In his latest pictures Velazquez seems to owe as little
as any man may to the example of earlier painters. But,
indeed, from the beginning he was a realist, and one
whose ideal of art was to use his own eyes. His early
pictures cannot be attached surely to any school; they are
of doubtful parentage, though, with some truth, one
might affiliate them to Caravaggio and the Italian naturalists. From the first, he shows sensitiveness to form, and
a taste for solid and direct painting. He quickly learnt
to model with surprising justness, but for a long time he
continued to treat a head in a group as he would if he
saw it alone. Only slowly he learnt to take the impression of a whole scene as the true motif of a picture. In
his early work he faithfully observed the relations between bits of his subject, but not always the relation of
each bit to the whole. If we compare the realistic work
of the young Velazquez with the pictures of the great
Venetians, we shall find it lacking their comfortable unity
of aspect. That aspect may have been more remote in
its relation to nature, but it was certainly ampler and
more decoratively beautiful. Up to the age of thirty, indeed, Velazquez seemed content to mature quietly his
powers of execution, without seeking to alter his style,
or to improve the quality of his realism. Had he died
during his first visit to Rome, it might have been

supposed, without absurdity, that he had said his last
word, and that, young as he was, he had lived to see his
art fully ripened. It would be difficult, indeed, to do anything finer, with piecemeal realism for an ideal, than the
later works of this first period. Pictures of the pre-Italian
epoch are 'The Water Carrier' (Apsley House), 'The
Adoration of the Magi' (Prado, 1166), 'Bust of Philip in
Armour' (Prado), full-length, 'Philip in Black' (Prado,
1182), and 'The Topers' (Prado, 1170). 'The Forge of
Vulcan' (Prado, 1171) was painted at Rome on the visit
which initiated the second manner.

The conversation and example of Rubens, the study of
Italian galleries, as well as the practice of palatial decoration at Buen Retiro, gave a decorative character to the
art of Velazquez in the second period. One tastes a flavour
of Venetian art in the subject-pictures, and one remarks
something bold, summary, and less intimate than usual,
about the portraiture of this time. As examples we may
take 'The Surrender of Breda' (Prado, 1172), 'The Boar
Hunt' (National Gallery), 'The Crucifixion' (Prado, 1167),
'Christ at the Pillar' (National Gallery), 'Prince Ferdinand',
with dog, gun and landscape background (Prado, 1186),
'The King as a Sportsman' (Prado, 1187), 'Don Balthasar
and Dogs' (Prado, 1189), the large equestrian 'Philip IV'
(Prado, 1178), the equestrian 'Don Balthasar' (Prado, 1180),
the equestrian 'Olivares' (Prado, 1181), 'The Sculptor
Montañés' (Prado, 1194). During these twenty years, if
ever, Velazquez relaxed his effort at naturalism—not that
he slackened his grip upon form, but that he seems to
have accepted in Italy the necessity for professional picture-
making. His colours became a shade more positive or
less bathed in light, and his unity to some extent an adopted decorative convention.

Upon his return from the second voyage, as if he had satisfied himself that Venetian art could not wholly render his manner of seeing, and that, at any rate, he had pushed it, in 'The Surrender of Breda', as far as it could go, he comes about once more and seeks for dignity and unity in the report of his own eyes. In fact, he adds the charm that we call impressionism to such work of the third period as 'Innocent the Tenth', done in Rome, 'Queen Mariana' (Prado, 1191), 'Las Meninas' (Prado, 1174), 'Las Hilanderas' (Prado, 1173), 'Æsop' (Prado, 1206), 'Moenippus' (Prado, 1207), the 'Infanta Margarita' (Prado, 1192),[1] 'Philip IV' (Prado, 1185), 'Philip IV Old' (National Gallery), and some of the Dwarfs and Imbeciles in the Prado.

Some sojourn in the capital of Spain is necessary if one would know the variety of Velazquez, and learn how often he forestalled the discoveries of recent schools of painting. Various stages of his growth, as shown in the Prado, remind us of various stages in the progress of modern naturalism. Sudden gusts of his fancy for some type or some quality in nature ally this or that canvas by Velazquez with the work of a man or a movement in our century. The names of Regnault, Manet, Carolus-Duran, Henner, Whistler and Sargent, rise to one's lips at every turn in the Prado; one thinks, but less inevitably, of Corot, when one sees the landscape of Velazquez. His early work recalls John Phillip and Wilkie, while the girl

[1] Stevenson refers to this portrait (Prado No. 1192) throughout his book under the mistaken identity of 'Maria Teresa' which Pedro de Madrazo had re-adopted on the strength of old inventory entries. It is, however, as Justi had already pointed out, a portrait of her half-sister, the Infanta Margarita, painted by Velazquez in 1660: the head and curtain are considered to have been completed by Mazo after his death. Stevenson greatly admired this picture, and quotes it constantly: its correct title has been substituted wherever it is referred to in the text.

in 'Las Hilanderas' should be the very ideal of art to the Pinwell, Walker and Macbeth school.[1] Except the 'Rokeby Venus',[2] the Prado lacks no picture essential to the full understanding of the painter's art. No other collection can give a just conception of the great works in Madrid. To see only the National Gallery, the Louvre, and the various private collections in England, leaves one without an adequate idea of the equestrian portraits, 'Philip IV', 'Olivares' and 'Don Balthasar'; 'The Surrender of Breda', 'The Sculptor Martínez Montañés', 'Moenippus', 'Æsop', the 'Infanta Margarita', 'Las Meninas', 'Las Hilanderas' and the series of Dwarfs and Imbeciles.

These pictures have changed very little; but, as with all old pigment, a good light is necessary to show the subtlety of the values and the expressive character of the subdued or suggested detail. Fortunately the light is excellent in the galleries of the Prado, which contain the principal pictures.

[1] John Phillip, R.A. (1817-67), the Aberdeen artist also known as 'Spanish' Phillip on account of his many pictures of Andalusian life and customs, was a great admirer of Velazquez and one of his earliest copyists in this country. The other artists here referred to are the Victorian academic genre painters G. J. Pinwell (1842-75), Frederick Walker (1840-75), and James Macbeth (1847-91).

[2] This celebrated picture did not enter the National Gallery until 1906, and Stevenson on more than one occasion refers to it as 'Mr. Morritt's Venus', meaning Mr. H. E. Morritt of Rokeby Hall, Yorkshire, the owner at the time. These references have been replaced in the text by the picture's modern title.

III

COMPARISON BETWEEN THE
THREE STAGES OF HIS ART

TRUSTING to report, and to the evidence of reproductions, I expected to find 'The Surrender of Breda' the finest Velazquez in the Prado. So I might have thought, if the painter's natural gift had been less explicitly set forth, if he had never lived to paint 'Las Meninas', 'The Spinners', 'Æsop', 'Moenippus' and the 'Infanta Margarita' (Prado). To some minds it is easier, and it is always quicker, to excel on the lines of older decorative conventions, than to start a new one on the expression of a personal view of beauty. From his early standpoint of the realistic painter, Velazquez first mounted to the position of great artist by excelling in the traditional cult of beauty; and it was only towards the end of his life that he divined a new art in the practice of personal impressionism. 'The Surrender of Breda' challenges the greatest masters on their own ground; it is unworthy neither of them nor of Velazquez, but for that very reason it is not the complete expression of the Velazquez eyesight. It was painted when he was scarce forty, and as an ornamental panel intended to co-operate with other historical works in the decoration of the *Salón de Reinos* of the Buen Retiro. Decoration hardly demands or permits of quick evolution or sudden novelty, and though the irrepressible

originality of the man still appears, it is evident that
Velazquez wisely attempted to follow the lead of his
favourite Venetian masters in the execution of this task.
And certainly he has succeeded, for the picture might be
hung in the Ducal Palace at Venice. But to realize such
an ambition was by-play, and not the work of Velazquez's
life.

If you would compare a realism, ennobled though somewhat chastened by grand decorative treatment, with a
realism not only exalted but intensified by the artistic
principles of impressionism, you have a fine opportunity
at the Prado. When you enter the long gallery from the
street, walk down it some way until you reach the Octagon Room; there you will see 'The Surrender of Breda',
and in a room nearby, 'Las Meninas', a work of the
painter's later life. 'The Surrender of Breda' you may
admire according to your nature; you may even consider
it the better picture, but by no means, as is 'Las Meninas',
an absolutely unique thing in the history of art.

As one views from a central standpoint the start and
finish of a race, so, from 'The Surrender of Breda', the
masterpiece of his middle life, you may look backwards
and forwards, upon the early and upon the late Velazquez.
It will not be forgotten that 'The Surrender of Breda' was
painted between the two voyages to Italy. As might be
expected, it agrees in many points with other canvases
painted during that period in which Velazquez was so
much occupied with palatial decoration. By its size, by
its freedom of touch, by the variety and warmth of its
colours, by the complexity of its pattern, by its dark foreground browns, by the quality of its blue distances, it is
allied to the large equestrian portraits, the hunting scenes
and hunting portraits of this period. Nor in its vigour

of brushing, and its force of positive colour, is it altogether unlike the 'Admiral Pulido' of our National Gallery and 'The Sculptor Montañés' of the Prado. The Admiral indeed is so unlike any portrait by Velazquez that some have doubted its authenticity, but it is very like the figures in 'The Surrender of Breda'.[1]

It is difficult to conceive that this great subject could be treated less conventionally without some loss of interest and dignity. No more than Veronese or Rubens, could Velazquez combine decorative splendour and historical clearness with the subtle mysteries of real tone and the impressionistic unity that lift truth into poetry. In other words, this kind of subject was unfitted to bring out the more original and characteristic qualities of Velazquez's genius. Subjects, however grand in title and dignified in historical association, are valuable to the painter in proportion as they give him a pretext for making the most of what is beautiful in his own art. No subject in itself can make or mar art; subject is indifferent except for its favourable or unfavourable effect on the artist. Even the record of a seen thing produces a noble or ignoble effect according as it records a grand or a trivial manner of using the eyesight, according as it shows a mean anxiety about details, petty circumstance and wiry pattern, or reveals sympathy with large shapes, subtle nuancing, or lovely qualities of paint. Let a bad painter call a figure by the name of what God he will, and carefully accompany it with sacred symbols, yet, if the forms are poor or ill-disposed, the figure remains a mean one, and less grand than the study of some street porter that is fuller of the

---

[1] The 'Admiral Pulido Pareja' (National Gallery No. 1315), of which there is another version at Woburn Abbey, is now definitely attributed to Mazo.

mystery of fine seeing and the emotions of a higher view of form. Remember, too, that what we call subject in painting imports still less than what we call subject in literature. This figure of the God and that of the street porter differ in title rather than in subject, for after all, the same model or true pictorial subject may have sat for both, and it is surely the grandeur of treatment, not the mere addition of symbols, accessories, and titles, that should make an essential difference between the two works.

It was perhaps, then, rather the purpose than the subject of 'The Surrender of Breda' which modified the art of Velazquez, and made it akin to the work of a Venetian. The canvas was to serve as a decorative panel, a thing to be looked at as one looks at a piece of tapestry; hence, doubtless, its decorative flatness, its variety of colours, its blue foundation, its brown foreground, and its block-like pattern of huge chunks of black and white and orange. It was scarcely the business of Velazquez to compact this broad but arbitrary illustration, explanatory of crowds, and costumes in a given situation, to adjust all this coloured accessory, to plant this hedge of pikes and lances against the distant landscape, to engineer the foreground so that the legs and their enclosed spaces might appear neither too distracting nor too utterly unlike the truth, to give some sense of space and distance but to give it gingerly, so as to bridge the great gulf between the main group and its background.

Yet how admirably it is done. Compare its stately figures with the coarse, dumpy men in 'The Repulse of the English at Cadiz', by Eugenio Caxés. Caxés follows his colleague Velazquez in his idea of colour, and in his view of the contending claims of open-air effect, decorative unity and historical fulness. But his reliefs are hard and even, his blocks of colour unfused, his drawing clumsy, and his whole picture duller, more spotty, and less arranged than 'The Surrender of Breda'.[1]   In colouring, in suavity of effect, that great Velazquez compares with any Titian. Its principal figures stand with as noble a bearing as any in painting. Spinola and Justin meet each other with gestures so poignant in expression, that they almost compel the nerves to involuntary imitation. Something of this dramatic aptness of gesture enlivens the series of large decorative panels which Rubens painted for the Luxembourg Palace. But the figures in the 'Reception of Marie de Medicis'[2] abound in courtliness and pomp, while the conqueror and the conquered of Breda, with a more human though a decently ceremonious stateliness, act out two of the most trying circumstances of life. The figures form the knot of an admirable composition, but this central interest is rather prepared by studied artifice than made important by the effect of a focused impression. Hence one is able to look at 'The Surrender of Breda' and imagine the centre cut out, and yet the chief sentiments of the picture preserved. The dignity of the two figures would be scarcely impaired by the omission of surroundings which, however well put in, yet exist for the purposes of illustrative and decorative arrangement.

Turn now to 'Las Meninas'. What a rounded vision swims in upon your eye, and occupies all the nervous force of the brain, all the effort of sight upon a single complete visual impression. One may look long before it crosses one's mind to think of any colour scheme, of tints

[1] See note 2, p. 57 above. The criticism seems a fair one, despite Zurbarán's now known authorship of this picture.

[2] The twenty-one pictures in the series 'The History of Marie de Medici' by Rubens, are now in the Louvre.

arbitrarily contrasted or harmonized, of masses balanced, of lines opposed or cunningly interwoven, of any of the tricks of the *métier*, however high and masterlike. The art of this thing—for it is full of art—is done for the first time, and so neither formal nor traditional. The admiration this picture raises is akin to the excitement caused by natural beauty; thought is suspended by something alike yet different from the enchantment of reality. This is not the reality obtained by the Pre-Raphaelite exploration of nature, which builds up a scene bit by bit, like the map of a new continent. The Pre-Raphaelite painter realizes the result of his separate observations no more than a geographer engaged on the survey of an unknown coast. He will not conceive of his picture as a big pattern which produces detail; he compiles a great many separate details, and accepts, though he has not designed, the ensemble which they happen to produce. Now the ensemble of 'Las Meninas' has been perceived in some high mood of impressionability, and has been imaginatively kept in view during the course of after-study. The realism of this picture is a revelation of the way the race has felt a scene of the kind during thousands of years. The unconscious habit of the eye, in estimating the relative importance of colours, forms, definitions, masses, sparkles, is revealed to us by the unequalled sensitiveness of this man's eyesight.

From our present point of view, 'The Topers' is even less real than 'The Surrender of Breda'. It belongs to a lower order of generalization. The mind that conceived it failed to grasp it except by successive acts of imagination. Its parts obey a purely formal instead of an impressional unity. The composition was, of course, designed to make a single pattern as to lines and masses, but the scene, with its modelling, colouring, atmosphere, and definitions, was never beheld as a whole vision in the mind's eye. Velazquez rose, I think, in 'The Surrender of Breda', to a higher art than he had dreamed of before he went to Italy. He reached at least a decorative unity, thought doubtless in so doing he sacrificed the poignancy of 'The Topers', which is due to a succession of climaxes. Each head is as strong as the best pair of eyes in the world could make it. If you can call it the highest art to take a number of powerfully-studied heads and sew them together to make a group, then 'The Topers' is as fine a picture as you want. But the unity of a work of art should be organic and pervasive, like the blood in a man's veins, which is carried down to his very toes.

As an art grows, everything that enters it becomes absorbed more and more into its constitution, and becomes a feature in a living organic unity. With the growth of music, composers felt the need of a more logical principle of unity, than a mere succession of separate phrases and climaxes; and as painting developed, painters began to comprehend other and more vital means of picture-making than the use of compelling lines and a formal composition. They had learnt that strong points in a picture kill each other, and that force in art is an affair of relation. They were to learn that there is a realistic as well as a decorative meaning in different breadths of treatment. The relative space and finish which a nose might arrogate to itself in a single head, must suffice for a whole face in a figure group, if due proportion and a reasonable width of view are to be preserved. A canvas should express a human outlook upon the world, and so it should represent an area possible to the attention; that is, it should subtend an angle of vision confined to certain

F

natural limits of expansion. Now, to group two or more
studies of figures in order to fill a larger canvas, either com-
mits the painter to a wider angle of vision, and consequently a more distributed attention, or else it compels
him to paint his group as if it were removed from him far
enough to subtend only the same angle as the single figure
of one of his previous studies. Let him choose either
alternative, and either way a difference of treatment is
forced upon him. This is a point which demands serious
study on the realistic grounds of perspective, modelling,
colour, and definition; but for the present it is sufficient to
settle it upon the merely decorative ground of complexity
of pattern. If a certain proportion of cutting up recom-
mends itself as beautiful and effective in any one sketch
or study, then unquestionably a compilation of such
studies must be a false method of composing a large canvas. The large canvas should not express a larger angle
of sight than the small one. In a word, the cutting up
of a canvas bears a ratio to the size of the canvas, and not
to the square foot of space. So that you may enlarge a
one-foot sketch, but you may not compile nine one-foot
studies to make a three-foot picture. Whether you compile actual separate sketches on one canvas, or merely
paint parts of that canvas under different impressions, the
fault is the same.

If there is anything in this unity of impression, 'The
Topers' is not the best picture in the world. We may
point to its prevailing tone of chocolate, and its hard,
staring, too equal force of definition, both faults the result
of compiled observations. Certainly, each head is a marvel of handling, of modelling, of character, but has this
handling or this modelling any beautiful dependence on
a great impression, or, as in 'Las Meninas', any relation

to the whole view embraced by the eye? On the contrary, one of those family arrangements in which several heads are separated by beadings, almost equally deserves the name of a picture. A Dutch portrait group, at any rate, claims quite an equal rank in the hierarchy of art. Rembrandt's 'Anatomy Lesson', Hals's and Van der Helst's figure groups, are on the same plane of realism, although some of them may be less powerfully executed than 'The Topers'.

Only a large mind takes a large view of a subject, and not without effort, too, whether the matter in question concerns art, philosophy, or practical life. For instance, the ordinary amateur of music likes short phrasing and a jerky emphasis, which makes the most of every accent, while the ordinary connoisseur comprehends and relishes the cheaper realism of the Dutch masters, but cannot easily grasp the broader truths of Velazquez. Small facts, shown by hard detail and strong, frequent contrast, are more easily perceived than the action of a principle which governs a whole scene. To many the finesse of Velazquez seems weakness, his atmosphere poor colour, his sense of natural arrangement, bad composition. These admirers of the Dutch realists would doubly admire Velazquez, if they could learn to see that he was not only cleverer but more sincere than Terborch,[1] Metsu, Gerard Dou, Nicolas Maes, or Van Ostade. These connoisseurs may not question the beauty of reality or the dignity of technique, but the first they assimilate only in little pieces, while they perceive only the immediate issues of the second. Quite

[1] There is an interesting affinity between the spatial relationships of Gerard Terborch (1617-81) and those of Velazquez. Terborch undoubtedly visited Madrid in the 1640s, as stated by Houbraken and by Johannes Roldanus in a poem of 1654 written on the occasion of the artist's marriage. See S. J. Gudlaugsson, *Gerard Terborch*, The Hague, 1959, (I) p. 38.

another objector to Velazquez is the man who says, 'What greatness is there in portraiture, and in the painting of common life, what can there be beyond "mere technique"?' For the moment we may bid him look again at the exquisite human feeling of 'Las Meninas'. Could the gracious attitudes of these bending maids, the calm born pride of the Infanta, the solemn gravity of the environment, speak more eloquently to us if this were an Adoration of somebody by an early and religious Italian? No, truly; but the mind of the literary objector, which will not obey the suggestion of paint, would then find itself, under the more familiar impulsion of words, running in an accustomed rut. Indeed, there is nothing lost in 'Las Meninas' of the natural forms, profound expression, and beautiful human sentiment of the Italian Pre-Raphaelites, while everything is gained in the way of a natural mystery of light, a true impressional unity of aspect, and a splendid perfection of technical resources. Nothing that art has ever won is wanting here unless it be composition by line, the charm of the nude figure, and the rhythmic swirl of Raphael's drawing. No great man is separable from his technique, and the difference between two great men lies largely in a difference of technique, for technique is truly the language of the eye. So that it may not be amiss now to speak of the technique of Velazquez—that is to say, of his composition, modelling, colour and handling. We have already compared three of his pictures, 'The Topers', a work of youth; 'The Surrender of Breda', a work of middle age; and 'Las Meninas', painted near the end of his life. In examining the technique of Velazquez we shall refer to these works, and shall describe others as occasion may arise.

IV

THE DIGNITY OF TECHNIQUE

IT is not the lover of pictures, but the devotee of his own spiritual emotions who needs to be told that technique is art; that it is as inseparable from art as features from facial expression, as body from soul in a world where force and matter seem inextricably entangled. In fact, the man who has no interest in technical questions has no interest in art; he loves it as those love you who profess only love for your soul. The concert-goers who disclaim any technical interest in music will be found to like a performance because they forget it in trains of thought about scenery, morals, or poetry. But one may walk on the hills to become healthy, or to escape crowds, and yet deserve no suspicion of a fondness for beauty. Under a mistaken conception of culture as the key of all the arts and sciences, intellectual people too often feel obliged to pretend an interest in arts for which they have no natural inclination. They insufficiently distinguish men born to take pleasure in the abstract and speculative from those born to love the concrete and sensuous—the black-and-white from the coloured mind. They cannot believe that the least taught ploughman whose senses are in tune with the pulse of nature may make a better artist than the man of loftiest thought who is encased in nerves insensitive to the quality of musical intervals or the character of

shapes and colours. The man of abstract mind apprehends
great ideas presented in the abstract medium of literature,
but in the concrete of painting he is easily deceived by
associations with words into spending his admiration on
mean forms, on foolish labour, on purposeless colour. He
looks at the merest pretence of modelling, at the coarsest
sham of colouring, at the contradiction of the whole by
the part, at the burial of beauty in niggling, and his dull
eyes accept the imposture on the recommendation of his
humbugged hearing.

The 'apostles of culture' grant but one gift—intellect—
to many-sided man, and accord but one faculty of imagination to the dweller in a house whose various windows
look down five separate avenues of sense. Often some
of these windows are blocked, and so many men must
misunderstand each other's reports of the external world,
but the man of culture too often keeps no window clean,
and from a dark chamber of the mind would explain to
everyone else the true inner meaning of what they see.
It is this prophet that despises technique because technique
differs as the material of each art differs—differs as marble,
pigments, musical notes and words differ. He hates
matter; because owing to matter the imagination in each
art is a gift whose absence cannot be compensated for
either by one of the other imaginations or by the abstract
intellect itself. Imagination in words is not imagination
in colour or form, as the cases of Turner and Goethe
amply prove. Without matter there is no art; without
matter there is no stuff in which imagination may create
an image. Sentiment is not imagination; spirituality is
not artistic feeling. We all cry, laugh, and put on airs;
we do not all imagine occasions and fashions of crying,
laughing, and striking attitudes. We feel the excitement

of a street fight, yet we cannot all come home and image that excitement as Dinet did in 'Une Bagarre',[1] with its tempestuous pattern of uplifted hands and swaying bodies quivering in an uncertain flicker of shadows and windy lamplight. It is a sensitiveness to the special qualities of some visible or audible medium of art which distinguishes the species artist from the genus man. We are all spirits; it is not in spirituality that the painter differs from us, but in that sensitive perception of visible character which enables him to imagine a picture all of a piece, all tending to express the same sentiment, all instinct and alive with feeling. Moreover, any difference that may exist between the material bases of the arts, exacts a corresponding difference between the qualities of temperament and imagination in the artists who practise them, also between the aims that are legitimate to the various arts, and between the feelings and laws by which works are to be judged and admired. Arts such as painting and sculpture, that appeal to the eye and display their contents simultaneously, differ vastly from those that unfold their matter to the ear in sequence. Painting and sculpture differ between themselves more slightly, and there is still less difference between pictures, whether realistic or decorative in aim, whether worked in oil or water, tint or line, monochrome or colour.

An art of space scarcely differs more from an art of time than one used purely from one mixed with representation of life, with utility or with symbolism. There is only one quite pure art—namely, symphonic music. Every shade of the complicated emotion in a symphony by Beethoven depends entirely upon technique—that is to

[1] Alphonse Etienne Dinet (1861-1929), pupil of Bouguereau and a well-known painter of Arab and oriental scenes.

say, upon the relations established amongst notes which are by themselves empty of all significance. The materials of other arts are more or less embarrassed in application by some enforced dependence on life. Words, since they serve as fixed counters or symbols, cannot be wholly wrenched from a determined meaning and suggestion; architecture satisfies a need of common life as well as an aesthetic craving, and painting not only weaves a purely decorative pattern, but also pretends to imitate the appearance of the world. None of these arts tranquilly pursue the beauties intrinsic to their medium; none circle in their orbit undisturbed; all upon examination appear to be, as it were, double stars, linked like Algol to a dark companion.

I might sum these statements in one or two principles. *First*, Art is not Life; for life is first-hand passionate emotion, while art deals with emotion second-hand, retrospective and disinterested. Life is variable, and a mixture of all materials—space, time, sound, colour, form, etc.; art is limited, partially controllable by the artist, and comparatively permanent. *Second*, Sentiment is not Imagination; for sentiment precedes art, and is common to all men, while imagination is a special power to arrange the material of some art in harmony with a mood. *Third*, There are as many separate faculties of imagination as there are separate mediums in which to conceive an image—clay, words, paint, notes of music. *Fourth*, The materials of the arts may be used with a double aim, or solely for their own direct and immediate qualities—as notes and intervals in music, which derive their character solely from the relations in which the artist chooses to place them; they have no fixed meaning, and a dominant and a tonic are interchangeable.

Our faith in any art reposes, however, upon the belief that its material, even if unavoidably adulterated with foreign significations, is nevertheless as capable as the sounds of music of expressing character in virtue of artistic arrangement. Otherwise, no medium of expression but the symphony should deserve the name of art. Now, as paint serves both to record impressions of the external world and to decorate a given space and shape, an artist, however partial to either, must give some measure of attention to each of these aims. He must study how the eye takes in nature, and how it takes pleasure in a canvas; and he must learn to reconcile these two ways of seeing when they disagree, as they sometimes may. When you look at nature, nothing remains absolutely fixed in appearance. Size, colour, pattern and proportion seem to fluctuate as you change your point of view, move your focus, widen or narrow your angle of vision. No object seems big but by relation to a smaller, no mass simple except when viewed as a whole in contrast to another, and no tone so bright that a brighter cannot make it dark. But when you see forms and colours set in the one plane of a picture, confined to its scale of pigment, and permanently bounded in size, proportion, and place by its four obstinate sides, then you see them fixed in unalterable relations, and always bound to express one and the same point of view. The laws by which one pictures an effect on the flat consequently differ from those that regulate ordinary sight. Many collocations of form or colour that please in a sunlit space of three dimensions with fluctuating borders become intensely disagreeable in a flat, framed panel. When he leaves nature for art, a man leaves bright boundless space where he has no dominion for a dark cloistered place where he is master—master of a medium susceptible of arrangement by harmony, contrast, and gradation; master to make his material speak in character, follow a vein of sentiment, express a mood of seeing. But he must learn to obey what, for want of a better word one may call the laws of decorative effect.

Plainly, then, there are two interests to be reconciled in a picture, the facts and impressions of nature on one hand, and, on the other, the beauties and exigencies of the framed pictorial world. A *modus vivendi* must be established between the imitative and the decorative, and the compact between these two may be called the convention of the art of painting. To object to the conventionality of art is to believe in absolute realism, which, if possible, would be a science and not an art. As things are, when you merely draw a line on an empty canvas you commit yourself to art, for you have given the line a positive character by placing it in some relation to the four sides of the canvas. To show a line quite unconditioned or uncomposed, one would require a canvas without limits—that is to say, nature. Convention, then, there must be, but it need not be rigid; it may vary with the impressions of artists, with the facts of nature, and with the characters of the mediums employed. The introduction of perspective, for instance, was a notable change in the convention of painting, since it implied a limitation in the use of our general knowledge of an object to what can be seen from one point of view. Different readings of the convention by men of genius give rise to various styles of painting, and successively attach a varying importance to the elements of technique as they deal with ideal form or real form, local colour or atmospheric, detail or general aspect.

This description of technique, compressed as it is of necessity, is intended for those who hate 'mere technique' and despise 'matter'. Matter does not level man with the beast or the stone; technique is not hateful, but only the point of view it expresses. There is a silly, unimpassioned mind which looks on nature without choice between things, which seems choked with trifles, which possesses no touchstone in its emotions wherewith to distinguish the important from the foolish. There may be such a thing as mere technique, but it is not what the vituperator of realism would have it. In words, it is nonsense verses; in paint, mere decorative consistency, without the meaning or emotion of truth to nature.

Technique in painting, then, must be understood as the method of using any medium of expression so as to bring out the character of a decorative pattern, or to convey the sentiment with which you regard some appearances of the external world. The two aims become one when the decorative pattern to be enforced is suggested by the mood in which you happen to look at your motif. If this be granted, then technique is as important to an art as the body to man. Both of them appear and act for two hidden questionable partners, sentiment and soul. Through them these silent invisible partners can speak with the outer world and influence the minds of men. When we would infer the soul of another man or the sentiment of a picture, we may do so only through the material senses and their analogies.

Technique, then, is the indivisible organic body of a man's conceptions, and cannot be rightly apprehended when studied in fragments. Yet, since the exigency of words forces us to present things in sequence, we must separate these living parts, and, as it were, dissect them dead. This necessity we will face, and will look separately at the qualities of Velazquez's technique —such as composition, colour, modelling and brush-work.

V

THE COMPOSITION OF VELAZQUEZ

WHEN he composed a picture Velazquez no longer relied altogether upon the arrangement by line or by colour blocks of the older masters; and when he drew anything it was not according to rule of thumb, canon of proportion, or even according to the later acquired knowledge of anatomy. He drew, as modern painters draw, almost entirely by eye, so that one thing was not more difficult to him to see rightly than another, and no receipts for representing thumbs, nails, curls, or other whole objects can be detected in his work. He wished any scene that he looked at in nature to be so treated in art as to express the quality and the distribution of the attention it had received from him in real life. Only thus could he hope to record the personal impressions which were his chief interest in the world. For this reason he did not look upon himself so much as an embroiderer of given spaces as a trimmer of spaces to fit given impressions. Perhaps the two ideas are comparable to the European and Japanese notions of dressing. Hence Velazquez when he painted nature held to no superstition concerning the accepted places for strong points in a canvas. Here was a scene which had imposed on him a certain impression of its character, and this view he felt bound to express by a shape of canvas that would

compose the scene as he had felt it. If, for instance, the
emotion of the scene had come from distributing the
attention in a vertical direction, he must have an upright
canvas, even in a figure group like 'Las Meninas'. This
was because to render the group as it had struck him it
was necessary to surround it with a certain sense of aerial
gloomy space, comparatively empty of incident, but not
of tone.

That same intention is manifested in Rembrandt's
'Supper at Emmaus' in the Louvre. The towering canopy
of the darkened vaults which overhangs the dimly lit
flickering table and the wavering figures completes the
impressional unity of the composition and heightens the
solemnity of the sentiment. I have often looked at 'The
Marriage at Cana in Galilee', by Veronese, in the Louvre,
but could never feel that the big space above the figures
was connected with them in any but the most formal
manner. These pillared galleries of marble, opening to
the blue sky, although they are incidents in the composition of the 'Marriage at Cana', scarcely seem to effect
the mood in which the artist regards his figure group.
They add no meaning to the general aspect of the group,
they cause no exaltation or depression of sentiment, they
affect the breadth of treatment not one whit, they operate
in no way upon the value of colours or the comparative
strength of definition. Therefore they are a mere literary
or explanatory note telling us that the scene took place
in certain surroundings, but not affecting the internal
treatment or sentiment of the figure group. On the other
hand, the vast gloomy top of 'Las Meninas', the empty
foreground of a Whistlerian etching, or the darkness of
a mysterious Rembrandt forms an essential part of a
picture and controls the force of colours and definitions,

explains the lighting and emphasizes the character of the sentiment which invests the figures. In fact, the surroundings of such pictures are as much part of the impression as the figures themselves; whereas it is impossible to say that the figures in the Veronese have been painted any differently owing to the presence of their surroundings or that they have been conceived as they would be seen in such a field of sight.

Modern painters have become quite accustomed to cutting and composing a scene in the interests of an impression rather than for the sake of mere decorative consistency. Yet each time that this necessity has led them out of the path of custom, especially when it led also outside of established decorative conventions, the public have wondered and have cried out at the eccentricity. It was so when Manet used a high horizon above the picture. It was so when Whistler left more than half his canvas, this time the lower half, bare and unpeopled by incident. Most people failed to perceive that it is sometimes impossible otherwise to show the difference between an object far off subtending a small angle of sight and the same object near at hand subtending a large angle. For the sake of dignity Corot at times consented to let this distinction remain doubtful, but his compliance has caused many to question the truth of his pictures. It will be found that Velazquez, while he revealed new truths about nature, scarcely ever forgot that a picture must be a dignified piece of decoration. But he certainly sought to attain beauty by methods somewhat unlike those employed by his predecessors.

Velazquez decorates a space by the use of tone more than any painter before him. Had Titian seen 'Las Meninas' he might have found the space filled inaptly, as far

s goes, by a row of heads crushed down into the
bottom of an empty canvas. And truly if you made a
drawing in line after the picture for Mr. Blackburn[1] it
would appear a poor composition. Even in a photograph
'Las Meninas' loses its rank among pictures, while on the
contrary the illustrated catalogues of modern exhibitions
frequently exalt a canvas to a position which its real
execution cannot maintain. Such pictures are often the
work of illustrators—that is, of men who conceive a composition in black and white, and, in painting, lose or bury
their original idea in new and irrelevant detail. 'Las Meninas' was imagined altogether as it exists in tone and colour;
it was seen in fact by the *tache*, to use a word of the early
impressionists, and the vision of it was not translated into
those lines which, if you remember, Delacroix neither
saw in nature nor wished to consider the sole source of
beauty in art.

An old master made all his space alive with a swirl of
flowing lines or built it compact like a monument with
blocks of balanced colour. Immense chunks of red, blue,
orange, white, brown, etc., are fitted into each other as
if they were the separate pieces of a puzzle. On this system each area of colour may require a different and separate
process of working to secure the quality of its tint or to
engage it in a semblance of chiaroscuro and effect. Such
preoccupations hamper the attainment of any unity except of line, of artificial harmony between darks and lights,
of decorative contrast between colours. Indeed, of the
mysteries and beauties of true tone which Velazquez explored in the heart of nature, and deemed proper to touch

[1] Henry Blackburn was, in Stevenson's time, the editor of illustrated
Notes on the Royal Academy. He was also the author of *Artistic Travel in
Normandy, Spain*, etc. 1892.

1. The Adoration of the Magi, 1619

Prado No. 1166

2. The Water Seller, *c.* 1621

Wellington Museum

3. Philip IV in Armour, *c.* 1625-28

Prado No. 1183

4. Philip IV in Youth, *c.* 1628

Prado No. 1182

5. The Topers, 1629

Prado No. 1170

6. The Forge of Vulcan, 1630

Prado No. 1171

7. Pablo de Valladolid, *c.* 1632-33

Prado No. 1198

8. Christ at the Pillar, *c.* 1631

National Gallery No. 1148

9. The Surrender of Breda, 1635

Prado No. 1172

10. Philip IV on Horseback, 1635-36

Prado No. 1178

11. The Sculptor, Martinez Montañés, *c.* 1636

Prado No. 1194

12. The Count-Duke of Olivares on Horseback, *c.* 1638

Prado No. 1181

13. The Boar Hunt, 1636-38

National Gallery No. 197

14. Æsop, c. 1640
Prado No. 1206

15. Moenippus, c. 1640
Prado No. 1207

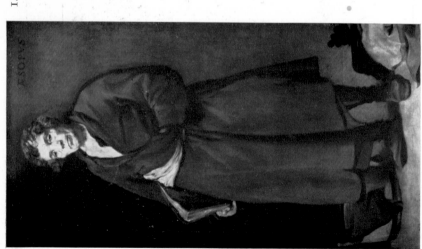

16. The Coronation of the Virgin, 1642

Prado No. 1168

17. The Dwarf 'El Primo', 1644

Prado No. 1201

18. The Rokeby Venus, *c.* 1650

National Gallery No. 2057

19. Queen Mariana of Austria, 1652

Prado No. 1191

20. Pope Innocent X, 1650

Palazzo Doria, Rome

21. The Garden of the Villa Medici, 1650 (?)

Prado No. 1210

22. Philip IV in Old Age, 1656

Prado No. 1185

23. Las Meninas, 1656

Prado No. 1174

24. The Spinners, 1657

Prado No. 1173

25. The Infanta Margarita, 1660

Prado No. 1192

man's emotional habits, these old men were comparatively ignorant, or, if they had an inkling of such things, they thought them altogether beside the question of art. The old masters' drawings, their numerous and careful cartoons, their very few notes of general effect, show their inborn love of space-filling by lines and definitely woven patterns. Their problem always being to fit the given space, they seldom sew pieces on to their canvases as Velazquez has done in many of his best pictures.

The life-size portrait of Philip IV in armour and on horseback (Prado), is a notable example of this practice. To each side of the canvas a strip three or four inches wide has been sewn, while, on the canvas itself, the pushing up of older contours reveals much correction and change of outline. This increase of the canvas by strips sewn on, common enough in the pictures of Velazquez, makes one think that he differed from his contemporaries in the way he set to work. You rarely meet with this habit amongst the men of the older decorative schools. They planned their picture beforehand, and approached it from a previous composition carefully calculated to occupy and decorate the given space. It seems possible that Velazquez began a picture in quite another spirit; that he conceived of it rather as an ensemble of tone than as a pattern of lines and tints. Unlike the older decorative artists, Velazquez has left few drawings. Probably he dashed in the main centre of the impression, and upon filling and darkening the rest of the canvas found sometimes that the centre required more elbow-room. In the Equestrian Philip the strips are not added to introduce any new feature or in any way to induce a change of place in the figure to one side or the other. They seem added simply to let the figure play in the centre of a

G

larger field. The dignity, the quality, the sense of artistry in the presentation of a thing depends very much upon its proportion to surroundings. So much around it, no more and no less, seems necessary to secure that it be seen under the conditions of sight which produced an impression on the painter, and which therefore must be reproduced to justify his treatment of the picture. It might be worth someone's time to inquire into the sewing together of these canvases, to hunt out some reason in each case, to unearth any half-buried tradition bearing on the question.[1] The main point seems to be that while unusual amongst the older men this habit is common enough amongst the moderns of whom Velazquez was a forerunner.

If you walk outside of Madrid upon the bare slopes facing the Sierras, you may see the reality which under-lies the Equestrian Portraits. Sit low down on the ground and you will have this same bare burnt foreground; should a figure pass, you will see the heavy blue of the distant hills low down behind its legs, while its head towers up into a cloudy sky. What he saw was endeared to Velaz-quez, and the arrangement of any one of his pictures carries with it the recollection of some actual occasion of sight. It is so with his portraits and with his subject-pictures. The two Philosophers, Æsop and Moenippus, stand as they might have stood scores of times in any room. Just so much space surrounds them as naturally falls under the eye; it is of the shape that best befits their shape, and it is furnished with accessory of no busier

[1] The addition of canvas strips to the equestrian portraits of Philip IV and Isabella, was to enable them to be fitted into position on the wall of the Salón de Reinos of the Buen Retiro Palace. Though Velazquez may have enlarged his canvases to give the subjects more air, it is more likely that he (or in some cases his successors) did so to convert portraits into matching pairs, utilize existing frames, or simply because canvas of the right width was difficult to obtain.

or more defined complication than the character of the impression demands. The canvases in these two portraits are remarkably tall and narrow, the heads in them almost touch the top of the frame, the colour is dark grey and atmospheric, while the general tone seems to bathe everything in a nuanced depth of distance and air. The aspect of the pictures in style and composition recalls many of Mr. Whistler's tall dark portraits wrapped in the mystery of gloomy interiors. Truth is the introducer that bids these two men shake hands across several centuries.

Velazquez you may say was never wantonly unusual; and, astonishing as his compositions may have looked to conventionalists, they appear to us to-day no more unnatural than nature, and much more natural than many modern experiments in art. In the arrangement of a picture by Velazquez there is always some intention to give the flavour of a particular impression, but at the same time a great effort to preserve the sane every-day aspect of nature. The fitting of a figure to its space always corresponds to the way it is supposed to be looked at, to the distance at which it is supposed to be seen, and to the number and complication of the accessories which share the dominion of the canvas. True, in his early work, such as 'The Adoration of the Kings', or even in the later 'Topers' and 'The Forge of Vulcan', Velazquez appears to compel things into unreasoned relation to each other, but this is the result of that realism which overlooks the general aspect of a view and studies the appearances of its separate parts. Composition in such a case cannot be said to influence the whole treatment of a canvas, but only its formal outlines. Drawing, modelling, definition of detail, balance of emptiness and fulness are determined in their character by successive study of pieces of the

picture instead of by a comprehensive view of the whole
subject. The faults induced by such technique are hardness, confusion, spottiness, and the sacrifice of the mystery
of enveloping air and light to petty markings and exaggerated spots of local colouring. It will be seen that
hardness, confusion, and spottiness can be corrected by
the sole influence of a noble decorative ideal, and that the
unrealistic combinations of Veronese, Titian, Rubens and
others are free from these defects. Yet their pictures cannot pretend to express fully the more subtle mysteries of
real light or to render an impression of the whole aspect
of an actual scene upon a painter's eye.

When we are absorbed in the work of any great man
whose art happens to express our own feelings, a natural
and not unseemly enthusiasm leads us to set him high
above all other artists; but in calmer moments we admit
no comparison between men who use technique to express quite different moods, sentiments, and perceptions.
You may as well compare Milton and Praxiteles as
Beethoven and Palestrina. Tonality is not more potent
and far-reaching in its effect upon modern music than real
lighting upon the arrangement of a picture. Both can
steep the commonplace in mystery, can flash a new meaning into old forms, can supersede worn-out conventions,
can electrify a dead passage, can sustain and bind together
a whole composition. Tone in a picture and tone in music
may not be better than the older methods of composition,
but they awake quite different feelings in the mind, and
so it is difficult to like the clarity of Palestrina and the rich
emotional tempest of Beethoven on the same evening, or
equally to appreciate in the same gallery the close solemn
tissue of a Velazquez and the arbitrary loosely-hung harmonies of the older schools. The Prado contains some

noble canvases by Titian, Rubens, Van Dyck, Tintoretto
and others, but to an eye that has dwelt long on the subtle
nuances of a Velazquez, they seem to fall to pieces or to
be held together only by the most palpable harmonic artifice. Yet there is art enough stowed away in 'Las Meninas',
as becomes evident when an engraver stumbles over the
hidden pitfalls that lie concealed beneath its suave surface.
Touch one of these many straight lines too firmly, miss
the nuancing of its accents, or tighten a detail of face or
costume, and some shrieking definition jumps at you like
a jack-in-the-box.

When you fail to grasp the ensemble of a Velazquez,
when you miss its profound and touching truth, you can
fall back on little else save a few disjointed facts of common realism. The art of the thing escapes you as the art
of a Beethoven symphony escapes the man who only
catches hold of occasional tag-ends of tunes hanging out
of a preposterous and tangled coil of sound.

Compared with those of Rubens, for instance, the pictures of Velazquez may seem grey, gloomy, and empty,
especially if one should be in that sensuous mood which
pardons everything for the sake of sumptuous decoration.
Let us think of a Rubens in the National Gallery, 'The
Rape of the Sabines', that flush-tide of the richest colour,
which positively seems to boil up in swirling eddies of
harmonious form. Its whole surface is swept by lines
which rush each other on like the rapid successive en-
trances of an excited *stretto*, till the violent movement
seems to undulate the entire pattern of the picture. Certainly examination proves the feeling due rather to decorative repetitions of line than to really striking actions
in the separate figures, yet the mind that has been possessed by this miracle of agitation may well find 'Las

Meninas' cold, empty and stiffly arranged. The colour of
Velazquez we must leave alone for the present, but the
exquisite precision and the eloquent breadth of the figures
in 'Las Meninas' surely weigh against the attractions of
a decorative consistency in the flow of lines. The breath-
ing of these young figures in their stiff clothes, the quality
of their flesh, the gait and bearing of them, the admirable
adjustment of the right lines of this grave chamber in the
old palace, legitimately appeal to the eye by an interest
of true pictorial art. The arrangement of this group,
which extends into depth and darkness, shows exactly
how it was felt in relation to its surroundings. These fields
of vibrating space, this vast shadowed top, wonderfully
modelled as it recedes from the eye, are no more empty
and useless around the figures than landscape itself, which
was so long withheld as uninteresting wasted space. The
rule was and still is that every space must co-operate in
the effect, but not necessarily by lines, agitated colours,
and defined forms. True, it may take one some time to
understand the part played by the top half of 'Las Meninas', but when one knows its gradations it appears as
grand a setting as the Alps.

When you are penetrated by the solemn statement of
'Las Meninas', even 'The Surrender of Breda' seems full
of a rhetorical if noble chattering, and to pass from a fine
Velazquez to any of the Italian pictures at the Prado is to
see them at great disadvantage. Not even 'The Assumption', by Titian (Academy, Venice), or 'The Transfiguration', by Raphael (Vatican, Rome), will quite content
those who want an art that fits the eye, who prefer a
natural and organic composition to a grand assemblage
of poses, draperies, wagging beards, contorted limbs, and
sweeping decorative lines. Few are the pictures that show

a unity embracing colour, definition, modelling, and tone as well as line—the unity of purpose that we find in 'The Last Supper' of Leonardo, in 'Las Hilanderas', 'The Rokeby Venus', and 'Las Meninas', in some Rembrandts, and in one or two works of recent and living painters. 'The Transfiguration' of Raphael could well bear translation into line, but no one will pretend that its chiaroscuro is affecting and mysterious, or its colour bound together by any principle beyond juxtaposition, repetition, and the compulsion of harmonious line. Its upper part, more-over, has no connection with its lower, except through symbolism. 'The Assumption', by Titian, although glo-rious in the power of its colour and the magnitude of its execution, scarcely answers to the finest ideal of picture-making. As a composition it is too patently broken into three parts. The upper group of the Father and Angels seems quite divided from the rest of the canvas, and in itself too dark, too distinctly cut out, too poorly en-wrapped, and altogether too unmysterious. The picture, indeed, pleases one better when the upper part is shaded out by the hand, and the top of the canvas is imagined to die out in mystery. As I was looking at it, I heard a lady say that it was a fine picture, but worldly, and that she did not like that great red figure in the front. This sounds ridiculous, as, if one dislikes the red drapery, one cannot like the picture, of which it is the very heart and vitals, yet without doubt her statement had some meaning. Prob-ably the sense of worldliness came from the hard definition of the top part, and the dislike of the gorgeous red and black harmony from the sacrifice of all subtleties of tone which such an explosion of colour demands.

To put all this in as few words as possible, it may be said that Velazquez uses tone as an important element in his composition; that, in fact, he utilizes the expression of space as well as the expression of form to give character to his picture. This is seen in the modelled depths of space that encase and permeate 'Las Meninas', 'The Spinners', 'The Rokeby Venus', the 'Æesop', the 'Moenippus', and the 'Infanta Margarita' (Prado). These we may call impressionistic compositions, while the earlier works, 'Adoration of the Kings', 'The Topers', 'The Forge of Vulcan' and others, we may call, in contradiction, realistic. 'The Adoration of the Kings' is opaque and dark, without a sense of space, either in the quality of the colour or in the arrangement of the picture. There is no room in its crowded composition, and there is no aerial suppleness in its tight lines and its comparatively small and hard modelling of surfaces. The pictures of Velazquez's middle life, as I have said, are decorative in aim, and the equestrian portraits of Philip IV, Olivares, and Don Balthasar resemble 'The Surrender of Breda'. The composition of these is very much freer and broader than that of the early pictures. Indeed, the canvases of this time are the only pictures which show anything of that scarcely definable air of pose and make-up which one expects in the true 'Old Master'. The hard, clumsy, over-detailed patterns of the dresses in the large equestrian portraits of Philip III and his wife Queen Margaret (Prado, 1176 and 1177), which might seem exceptions, are not the work of Velazquez.[1] He found these portraits already executed,

[1] All authorities are agreed that Velazquez was only partially responsible for these two equestrian portraits (and for that of Queen Isabella), but the exact degree of his participation, and the chronology of it, are still unsettled. The theory that he re-modelled earlier originals by Bartolomé González (d. 1627) now tends to find less favour than the suggestion that he himself planned them, left much of the execution to assistants during his absence in Italy, and finally revised them for the Buen Retiro Palace on his return.

and merely touched them up in his own broader and more vigorous style. The pattern of the queen's dress is plastered in with little regard to the perspective of folds or the changing value of lights. It is interesting to compare its awkwardness in the composition with the beautiful ease of patterns worked by Velazquez himself, as, for instance, those in 'The Infanta Margarita', or in the Dwarf with a large dog.[1] The queen's dress is worked in the mechanically detailed style of work, which can be seen in pictures by Sanchez Coello and other predecessors of Velazquez.

From what has been already said, backed by a glance at the illustrations to this book, it may be seen that Velazquez relied very seldom upon parallelism of lines, whirlpools of curves leading the eye to a centre, or, indeed, upon any other of the many traditional resources of composition. But it would be narrow-minded to blame either the composers by line or the composers by spot. Different ends justify different means in each case, and, moreover, composers, like cooks, although they have principles, apply them ultimately in practice at the dictation of taste. You cannot easily convert people on matters of real taste— decide how much sugar they can absorb without cloying their palates, or how much balance and symmetry of arrangement they can stand in a picture without feeling sick at its artificiality. The work of Claude affords an example of formal, rhythmic composition which has proved distasteful of late days to many who still admire

---

[1] The portrait of a Dwarf with a large dog, (Prado No. 1203) was formerly wrongly believed to be 'Antonio el Inglés', a buffoon who died in 1617, before Velazquez came to Court. Though it has generally been accepted in the catalogues as an autograph work, doubts have been recently cast on its authenticity (see the article by J. López-Rey cited in the Bibliography). Stevenson, however, refers to it on more than one occasion as an example of late Velazquez brush-work.

its colour. What is stranger still, some lovers of Wagner now find the melody of Mozart too formal, too simple, too evident. But while radical and physiological differences of taste unquestionably exist, we must not be too ready to accept blame due to partial blindness, or mere unfamiliarity with new conditions, as the result of an unconquerable physical aversion. When impressionists have depicted figures looked at from above they have been told that their pictures were unnatural by those accustomed to see people painted on a studio throne. But when it was first introduced did even perspective look natural, or did it require custom to familiarize the eye with its curious forms? Artists should not be censured for their admitted carelessness of public opinion, as the most natural view looks unfamiliar to creatures of habit, just as to a conventional society a realistic representation of human passions appears madness. In such a matter of taste as the point at which a canvas becomes over-spotty can one pronounce with certainty? There is a boiling point on the thermometer; is there a cutting-up point which determines the ratio to the area in which you may subdivide a picture? Here are two reasons why no one can lay down the law with assurance. *First*, the point of spottiness greatly depends on whether the eye habitually takes heed consciously of a large or a small field of vision. *Second*, a dangerous complexity of detail and matter in a picture may be rendered comprehensible and orderly by rhythm in the design, but then the spectator must be able to embrace the extent and meaning of this harmonious arrangement.

Velazquez relies on tone, on the magic of true light, on delicate adjustments of proportion between masses to unite the many figures of 'The Spinners' and 'Las Meninas'. As to harmonious lines, he trusts to them in composing a picture as little as he trusts to defined lines in his rendering of form. He never cuts up a figure or face by lines drawn round the eyes, lips, or other features; he gives a sense of intimacy by gradations of tone rather than by fixed contours. Thus, while a painted Holbein differs very little in method and aim from a Holbein drawing on white paper, a picture by Velazquez belongs altogether to another branch of art.

Harmonious line may often cover bad composition of tone, colour, or mass, just as the wonderful tone of Velazquez may at times dignify very ordinary line. For instance, the line weavers constantly run two or three pictures into one frame, so that if you neglect their lines their composition-masses of tone appear meaningless and spotty. If a painter looks at one corner of the canvas exclusively he is apt to put a smaller frame round it mentally, and so make a fresh set of composition masses out of what was only the subordinate detail of the original *motif*. Of this fault Velazquez, at least in his later work, is never guilty.

Within the scope of Velazquez's own work, and even of his later work, the difference between Italian traditional composition and the new impressionistic composition may be easily illustrated. The 'Coronation of the Virgin' (Prado, 1168) is arranged upon the system of balanced blocks of colour and harmonious play of lines. But I have no doubt that even in this picture a purist in old mastery would object to the direction of the cherub's wings, which point out of the picture and downwards, instead of in and upwards. A man who composes best by tone abandons nature at some peril, when, as here, he undertakes to show purely ideal circumstances.

In the case of 'Las Meninas' and 'The Spinners', Velazquez unquestionably worked from nature. Indeed, there
is in this country a large study of 'Las Meninas', four feet
wide. It belongs to Mr. Ralph Bankes of Kingston Lacy,
and only differs from the larger picture in that the king
and queen are not reflected in the mirror at the end of
the room, beside the open door.[1] It is generally said that
Velazquez was painting the king, who sat in the spot from
which the spectator is supposed to see the picture of 'Las
Meninas'. During a moment's rest the Infanta came in
with her attendants, and the king was struck with the
group which fell together before his eyes. Near him he
saw the princess, her maids, her dog, and her dwarfs;
a little farther on the left, Velazquez, who had stepped
back to look at his picture; farther still on the right a
duenna and courtier talking; while at the distant end of
the gallery the king saw his queen and himself reflected
in a mirror, and, through the open door, Don Joseph Nieto
drawing back a curtain. The canvas shown in the picture
would naturally be the one on which Velazquez was
painting the king's portrait. Some, however, will have
it to be the very canvas of 'Las Meninas', which Velazquez
was painting from a reflection in a mirror placed near to
where the king had been sitting. The perspective in the

[1] The Kingston Lacy study for 'Las Meninas' was illustrated by Stevenson in the first edition (1895) of his book (Pantorba therefore is in error in
stating in his 1955 Catalogue that it has never been published). It measures
56 × 48 inches and differs slightly from the original as regards the reflections
in the mirror and the background figure of Nieto. The picture was
bought about 1811 from the heirs of the Spanish critic Jovellanos, who in
1789 had written an essay claiming it as the original sketch. Recent writers,
however, have tended either to ignore it or to dismiss it as a copy. As
Sánchez Cantón says, 'in modern times it has become a picture without
a literature: similar misfortune has befallen other presumed sketches of
Velazquez: none of them have been accepted by the most authoritative
critics'. (*Las Meninas y sus Personajes*, 1952, p. 33.)

picture hardly seems to agree with this view, but rather makes Velazquez to have been working on the king's right hand. It is not a matter of importance, and the story of the conception of the picture may easily have got mixed in the telling. It is just possible that Velazquez was painting, or was about to paint, a portrait of the Infanta only, when the idea of the large picture suddenly occurred to him or to the king. The canvas of 'Las Meninas' is made of separate pieces sewn together, and one of these just contains the Infanta, with room for accessories or a subordinate figure. Another tradition says that the red cross of Santiago, which you can see on the painter's breast, was painted there by the king's own hand, as a promise of the honour that was to be conferred on him afterwards.[1]

'Las Hilanderas', or the spinners in the royal manufactory of tapestry, was painted later than 'Las Meninas', which it resembles in one or two points.[2] In both pictures the top runs up into gloom, though the vaulted chamber of 'The Spinners' does not tower up and dominate the composition so much as the upper part of 'Las Meninas'. Both pictures are conceived in tone and steeped in the mystery of light, and 'The Spinners', in a higher degree, is cheered, in the midst of its deepest gloom, by a vista opening at the back into a brilliantly-lighted space. But in 'The Spinners' the texture of illuminated

[1] The story that the King himself painted the Cross of Santiago (which also figures in the Kingston Lacy picture) on Velazquez's breast is a pleasant one but probably apocryphal. 'Las Meninas' was painted in 1656, and Velazquez was not proposed for the Order until 1658, the actual ceremony of investiture taking place in November 1659.

[2] 'Las Hilanderas' is now known to have a mythological content based on the fable of Arachne, who was changed into a spider by Pallas for having woven a tapestry depicting the rape of Europa by Jupiter. For some of the extensive literature on this picture, see the bibliography.

and shadowed air is richer and more varied, it clothes a greater variety of forms, it fuses a wider variety of tints, a range of stronger local colours. In keeping with its more lively colour scheme, the composition lines of 'The Spinners' flow more sinuously and harmoniously than the rigid forms of 'Las Meninas', and the masses twine and interweave in a more rhythmic and balanced pattern. 'Las Meninas' is graver, nobler, and more imposing, also less expected, less formal, and less aided by artificial elegancies of arrangement. 'Las Hilanderas' is more supple and insinuating in its grace of pattern, more enchanting and varied in its treatment of colour and detail.

In both pictures Velazquez is shown at his best. He copes with the most difficult problems of modern impressionism; he works them out on a large scale, and he pushes the rendering of his conception in each case to the furthest possible completion. One or two smaller pictures, single figures or heads, may perhaps compare in modelling, in expression of light, or in quality of colour, with these two great masterpieces just mentioned, but on the score of composition not even the supple and flowing 'Rokeby Venus', the 'Christ at the Pillar' of our National Gallery, or 'Æsop', 'Moenippus', 'The Infanta Margarita' and others in the Prado, can rival the importance of 'Las Meninas' and 'The Spinners'. It will be well, therefore, to speak of smaller pictures after dealing with colour and modelling, and at present to pass on to the landscape art of Velazquez.

In this branch of painting the large upright 'Avenue of the Queen', at Aranjuez (Prado), is enough to make us proclaim Velazquez a modern and an impressionist, when we think of the contemporary Claude and Poussin. The view is seen from a height outside the avenue so that the

horizon is half-way up the canvas, and the avenue occupies only the right-hand side of the picture. On the left
you see the Tagus bounded by a hedge of distant trees,
surmounted by an evening sky. This scarcely promises
much dignity of arrangement, and yet the picture is fuller
of grandeur and immensity than any I can remember.
The trees in two tall towers of gloom, rise into a blue sky
streaked with floating filaments of cloud, while on the
dusty road below, coaches and cavaliers, like a string of
insects, cross the brown empty foreground and plunge
into the deep recesses of the avenue. The canvas is a large
one for landscape, and it is treated throughout with a
breadth of style proportionate to the size of the composition, and suitable to the implied distance of the spectator from the frame. The manner of seeing recalls the
work of both Corot and Whistler, though neither of these
painters ever saw it. In this picture, as in his other open-
air works, Velazquez has cut the scene out of nature in
a personal manner, so as to fit his sentiment about the
place. He has insured the harmony of smaller details,
both in tone and line, by swamping accidental or contra-
dictory forms such as the saw-like edges of trees, or accidental and distracting holes of light in the darker depths
of shades. This picture and the 'Fountain of the Tritons'
(Prado, 1213), another view at Aranjuez, belong to the
latest period of Velazquez's life.[1] The fountain is notable
for the soft, feathery handling of the trees which veil the
sky; the figures seem out of scale, and Carl Justi con-
siders them additions by J. B. del Mazo, son-in-law and
pupil of Velazquez. Other landscapes, such as the two

[1] The 'Calle de la Reina' at Aranjuez is now considered to be a work
of Mazo, and the 'Fuente de los Tritones' to be substantially by Velazquez
except for the out-of-scale foreground figures which (as Justi suggested)
are probably by Mazo.

finely-handled sketches of scenes in the 'Villa Medici', belong to the first visit to Rome in 1630.[1]

In landscapes, as in his figure-subjects, Velazquez does not seek ideal beauties or acceptably grand, poetic, religious, and picturesque *motifs*. He takes a chunk of nature and can do without Florentine trees, rocky hills, flowers and castles; he frames a slice of life and forgoes hoods, halos, and the paraphernalia of ecclesiastical sentiment. The thing that he paints has a flavour of its own; owing to a hazard of nature, owing to an accident of the way he himself looks, the scene charms him by the play of light on colours, or by some subtle relation among proportions which gives grandeur, delicacy, or an air of captivating greatness.

Of many qualities possible to painting and useful in composition, proportion is at once the most enduring in its effect, and the most unobtrusive in its compulsion on the eye. Some qualities exact a strained and conscious effort of appreciation; their full expression in a picture demands a full attention from the spectator. Now a work of art should charm us both when we examine it and when we dream over it half-consciously. Certain efforts of draughtsmanship, for instance, require study, and appeal to an intelligent, wide-awake interest in action, anatomy, and things beyond the immediate presence of the canvas. The subordination by harmony of complicated elements can only be fairly enjoyed by an intellectual combined with an intuitive operation. Mere contrast of colour sets

---

[1] There is still no complete agreement as to whether the two Villa Medici landscapes were painted during the first (1630) or the second (1650) Italian visit. It was formerly presumed, owing to their freedom of treatment, that they dated from the latter, but the less rigid stylistic chronology now being adopted tends to favour the first visit, especially as Velazquez lived at the villa during that period.

the nerves on the *qui vive*; it challenges criticism, it awakes the caprices of the individual taste.   Balance asks to be weighed; geometrical relations set the spectator measuring.   Proportion, like a fine day, puts us into a pleasurable frame of mind without conscious effort on our part.   An unlearned man may look at a Greek temple and be pleased without recognizing it to be a work of art.   He may not feel any interest in it or any wish to examine or inquire, but his nerves are cheered or soothed as by woods, seas or mountains.   Fine proportion always seems to have grown up naturally, it shows none of the difficulties that have been painfully overcome, none of the snares of annoyance, that have been skilfully avoided.   Proportion cannot be done by rule; it is experimental and intuitive, and its effect, however potent, is unintellectual.   To make it by law is to copy mechanically.   The proportions of the Parthenon are for the Parthenon, and must be changed for another building.   Of course, space-fillers use proportion, but oftener a more or less imitable harmony of lines; Velazquez oftener proportion.   Hence his art is less evident, less exciting at first, and less fatiguing afterwards. The more you know his work the more you see in it, and what appeared the most wonderful effort of artless realism becomes the most consummate finesse of art.

H

VI

HIS COLOUR

PERSONAL taste counts for much in the whole field of art, and nowhere so much as in colour. Whether we think of the painter or the onlooker, whether we think of making or admiring a picture, it is equally impossible to lay down hard and fast rules of practice, and to discriminate between good and bad with scientific certainty. A native tendency decides for us what kind of use we shall make of colour—a difference in eyes, early habits, instinctive preferences, causes one man to feel elation at the rich extravagance of Venetian colour, and another man to be touched by the natural poetry and sober dignity of a fine Velazquez. As this is so, I need scarcely apologize for speaking of my own feelings; art is meaningless without personality and its action can only be studied in its effect upon oneself.

As a child I was fond of engravings after certain pictures, but when I saw some of the originals I was astonished that the painter should have spoilt the nobility of his work by staining it with unnaturally bright and spotty colouring. The breadth and solemnity of the black and white had disappeared, like the grandeur of a figure when it is tricked out in tinsel and motley. Yet I can remember that I was pleased with bright colour in the real world, and now I can put my finger on some of the reasons for these apparently

inconsistent tastes. In nature a vivid tint appeared only
as a rare splash, which set off by contrast the charm
of the prevailing sheet of soft silvery iridescence, or im-
palpable umbery warmth that veils and reveals objects in
the chiaroscuro of real light. To show strong colour thus
governed by the tone of the ensemble is not the same thing
as to play with strong colour in an artificial scheme of
decorative harmonies, and you may count on your fingers
the men who have done it with success. The black and
white medium and the Venetian glow, different as they
are, agree in being quite arbitrary expressions of the combined effect of colour and light. As all art is convention,
I merely mark the difference between such forms of art
and naturalism without implying anything of praise or
blame. The man who sees the world through tone, who
feels the beauty of colour mainly in its relations to this
prevailing principle of tone, cannot easily appreciate a use
of colour which neither frankly abandons nature nor treats
the mystery of real lighting with poetic insight. Brought
up, as a boy, on Mr. Holman Hunt, Sir N. Paton, and the
Scottish Academy,[1] I soon concluded that I congenitally disliked paint. However, in later days at Fontainebleau, I became intimate with Auguste Ortmans, a painter to whom
the Emperor had given a studio in the château. When
the Empress was away he showed me her Corots;[2] he took
me to see work at Barbizon; he set me to paint in the
forest, and I learnt that colour was not necessarily a blazing falsity. Then schools of art overwhelmed me, and
face to face with the difficulties of nature I was led off my

[1] Sir Joseph Noel Paton, R.S.A. (1821-1901), painter of fairy scenes,
and a leader of the group of Scottish Academicians.

[2] One of these Corots was doubtless the famous 'Souvenir de Mortefontaine', painted in 1864, which hung at Fontainebleau until it entered
the Louvre in 1889.

legs, and, as usual, forgot how the world really looked to me whilst I was prying into the drawing, modelling, and local colouring of its interesting corners. Being impressed does not imply the imagination to recreate, otherwise we might very much multiply the number of good artists.

There must be some who feel with me that many bright colours of extreme chromatic difference confound the perception of tone, and give the picture an air of insincerity, shallow pomp, and decorative flashiness. The solemn mystery of nature is lost for the sake of a costumier's taste for courtly splendour.

You cannot easily bridge over the difference of taste which leads one man to enjoy the subtle modification of colour by light, and another to revel in the bright untrammelled play of colour used decoratively. The decorative end may be attained gloriously, and by a triumph of art as in the case of the Venetians, but to people of my sort it remains a triumph of artifice, not a great victory of the emotions. We are reconciled to it slowly and not until we have learnt enough to perceive and to be awestruck by a skill which at first escaped our ignorance. But the miracle does not repose on the basis of our own feelings nor conciliate the testimony of our eyes. It seems unphilosophic and without roots in the life we lead. It cannot touch the old associations of our race with reality, or pull upon nerves that have been fashioned by the emotions of a thousand generations. Now, great work to those who make it and to those who feel a vital sympathy with it never appears wholly decorative in aim. In proportion to our native blindness or aversion to the point of view taken, so the decorative aim seems to preponderate over the natural or realistic. To some men, Whistler seems to blot out nature in arbitrary fuliginousness when he

meant to coax beauty out of the heart of what he saw.
To some, Velazquez appears to be a decorator with an
unaccountable taste for certain cold harmonies of a restrained kind, turning upon black and grey, which he
manages to manipulate with some cleverness. To me,
again, he is nothing of the sort, and now that he has shown
me the way, I can see a Velazquez wherever I please.

To the unthinking, colour is absolute, and its quality
in every case inherent to each particular tint. It is impossible here to argue against such a conviction, but one may
point to the blue complementary shadows on white chalk,
and to the effect of coloured clothes on people's com-
plexions. I have observed that a piece of coarse green
pastel which made a dark mark against the foreground
grass of a freshly-painted landscape, relieved as a light spot
against the apparently blue and ethereal sky of a Claude.
Such is the power of the relations within the range of a
key. When we call a single colour beautiful or ugly we
unconsciously compare it with the general hue of nature
as a background.

It follows from the interdependence of colours and from
the compelling power of key relations, that whether we
look at imitative pictures, decorative patterns, or natural
scenes, we shall see colours differently, according as it is
our habit to embrace large or small fields of sight under
one impression. You may choose a wall-paper in bed
from a two-foot pattern close at hand, and experience
some surprise when you see it hung on an empty thirty-
foot wall. So, when the primitive realist tints small
separate objects by a process as near matching as possible,
we cannot wonder that his picture, which contains some
hundreds of such matches, should look unnatural. A
realist of broader perceptions compares the effect of colour

against colour, while the impressionist notes or imagines the general tone of the whole field which he paints, and then determines the quality and value of spots by their relation to this perceived ensemble. These ways of looking give rise to quite different sentiments about external nature.

In all kinds of really artistic work, whether decorative, realistic, or impressionist, one sees evidence of that liking for unity of some kind, which pervades every art. In painting it may appear in line, chiaroscuro, colour, or in a combination of all these qualities. An inborn sense of decorative colour seems to recommend a unity of richness, in fact a kind of varnished glow, to the natural man. You see it in the love for reflections, particularly in rather dirty water, in the taste for Claude Lorraine glasses, in the passion for the old varnish that softens the hues of a picture and solves them in a warm and luscious juice. The world in general admires the harmonizing effect of time upon the tints of a picture, and the artist of a decorative turn of mind has been greatly influenced by the beauty of old colour. Nevertheless, the lover of nature feels cheated of dear and familiar emotions when he sees some arbitrary decorative principle employed to effect this much-desired fusion of colours. It may become the decorator to conceive a scheme of colouring, but it behoves the naturalist to find in nature the bond that will unite and beautify colour. In this case, of course, one means by nature the man's impression of the colour-effect of the whole field of vision about to be painted. In virtue of this impressionistic way of seeing, an artist gives his pictures a unity of colour which is significant as well as decorative in its beauty. Now, it is evident that much of the significance of such colour will be lost to eyes that habitually take in a smaller field of impression than is taken by the painter. Thus, there are many people to whom the colouring of a Velazquez looks cold, dry, and inexplicably grey. Velazquez aimed at the cool effect of silvery light, and if you look at the ensemble of his picture as he looked at nature, you will rarely see a poor passage of colour.

No pictures maintain such a close unity of key as those of Velazquez. But this close unity of key corresponds to a real perception of nature. When a lady in a brightly-coloured hat passes one of his canvases, it is true that you see the whole picture of one tone in contrast to the hat. Yet the key is so subtly varied, so delicately nuanced, that the picture, unless through such a contrast, appears to be a luminous tissue of air, not definitely red, green, black, or yellow. But 'Las Meninas', even when subjected to this test of contrast with real people sitting on a bench before it, preserves its appearance of truth and natural vigour. Its colour relations continue to look as subtle and as naturally complex as before; and when you look at both nature and the picture, your eye only seems to pass from one room into another. The sense of space and roundness in the real room is not greater than in the painted room. On the other hand, contrast with the real world exposes no exaggerated reliefs, no over-trenchant definitions, no false lighting in 'Las Meninas'. It is, in fact, neither too tame nor too swaggering and theatrical in its treatment of natural appearances. When purely decorative, a close unity of key may sometimes result in the case of old pictures from age and varnish, and only sometimes from the painter's intention, while in the case of modern work it occasionally comes from a palpable dis-illusionizing glaze of warm colour sloshed over crudity of value. The pictures of Velazquez, though a little duller than they were, have changed less than those of most painters, and they show no traces of glazing or saucing; indeed, they are among the few old pictures that have not gained by time.

The general principle which unites the colours of his later pictures was reached by Velazquez, neither through that feeling for decorative fitness which governed the work of his middle period nor entirely through the inborn Spanish love of dark hues that we see in Ribera. It comes from a broader and more imaginative outlook upon the values of colour as they are affected by juxtaposition, by atmospheric conditions, and, above all, by their inclination to the source of light. This view of the aspect of nature led him to study not only black and white but chromatic tone. A change of the plane on which a colour lies tends to make it not only lighter or darker, but to change its hue—to dose it with some proportions of blue, yellow or red. Velazquez recreates the aspect of a place and its conditions of lighting so convincingly that one feels able to imagine the value which any local tint would receive if introduced into any position in the picture. True, he seldom chooses a subject from nature which contains many bright local tints, but he always treats those he admits with a perfect mastery of the resources of colour. He is as subtle a colourist as real light itself, which veils even a monochromatic subject in a dress of coloured tissue. Indeed, the delicate colourist is never better proved than when he would paint the chromatic nuances of light upon a *motif* whose chief local tints are black or white. By his treatment of blacks in such pictures as 'Moenippus', 'Philip IV Old' (Prado) and 'The Sculptor Montañés', Velazquez amply demonstrates the amazing finesse of his eye.

The beggar Moenippus in his faded black cloak, towers

up to the top of the narrow canvas which represents him
standing, with a book and jar at his feet, against the bare
grey wall of a dim and dusty garret. A great shadow
wraps the feet; but, above, the figure is tilted back on the
hip somewhat after the manner of Mr. Whistler's 'Lady
Archibald Campbell'. Thus a discreet light skims the
upper half of the man, gently silvering the rusty black
and revealing the shape of the shoulder and the character
of the pose. The beauty of this passage of colour becomes
more patent if one notes the different quality of the black
in 'Portrait of a Man' (Prado, 810) by Greco (1548-1614),
who painted portraits in Spain before the days of Velazquez. Greco opens a pit or hole of black asphalt; Velazquez
flushes the blacks of Moenippus with a hundred nuances
of greenish light. Although he could see the finest shades
of distinction in dark tones, Velazquez was no colourist in
the eyes of those who see little difference between black,
Van Dyke brown, or Prussian blue until they are plenti-
fully diluted with white. These men are the drunkards
of colour. We will not deny that they like it; both the
gourmet and the *gourmand* may be said to like food and yet
we give them by no means an equal reputation for taste.

In the early full-length 'Don Carlos' (Prado, 1188) by
Velazquez, the blacks compared with those in the 'Moenippus' look hard, unaerial, and scarcely obedient to the
light. This comparison of the early and late treatment of
local blacks by Velazquez may be paralleled by a comparison of his general colour in the first period and in the
last. 'The Forge of Vulcan', dating from about 1630, the
end of the first period, is, as it were, conveyed in a vehicle
of brown, not at all luminous and aerial as the atmosphere
of the later silvery works, 'The Spinners', 'Las Meninas',
'The Rokeby Venus', 'Moenippus', 'Philip IV in Old Age'

and 'The Infanta Margarita'. This brown of the 'Vulcan'
is an almost monochromatic tissue of tone which accom-
panies and unites the colour of the picture. It is almost
as positive as the brown bituminous vehicle used some
twenty years ago by persons supposed to have been edu-
cated at Munich. Few strong local tints are embedded in
the brown tone of the 'Vulcan'; you have nothing in the
subject more chromatic than the flesh tints of the dark
blacksmiths, and the lighter ones of Apollo, a yellow
drapery, and, on the anvil, one spot of glowing iron. The
rest of the picture consists of originally greyish colours,
drowned in a brown vehicle. It is curious, by the way,
that the angel in 'Christ at the Pillar' (National Gallery,
date 1639) is the same person or the same type of person
as the Apollo in the 'Vulcan' of 1630. The National Gallery picture is greyer and more silvery than the 'Vulcan',
but it still shows something of the dryness and hardness
which was to be entirely abandoned in the last period.[1]

Vivid colours occur now and again in the subjects chosen
by Velazquez, as, for instance, the pink scarf in 'The Equestrian Philip', the draperies, etc., in 'The Coronation of the
Virgin' (Prado, 1168), the red cloth in 'The Rokeby Venus',
the curtain and the tapestry in 'The Spinners', and touches
of rose and red in 'The Infanta Margarita' (Prado), but they
are certainly not frequent. The 'Coronation of the Virgin', though painted in the third period, is of a conventional Italian style in its composition;[2] and it is not

[1] The 'Christ at the Pillar' (National Gallery No. 1148) is now dated
rather earlier, c. 1631-32, during, or very soon after, the first Italian visit,
thus further strengthening the relationship with 'The Forge of Vulcan'.

[2] 'The Coronation of the Virgin' is now considered to have been painted
c. 1641-42, i.e. during Velazquez's second period, as there is a copy with
variants by Jusepe Martínez, painted in 1644. The colouring of this picture, which recalls El Greco, has always greatly exercised the attention of
critics.

surprising that a picture with fluttering draperies, rounded clouds, cherub heads, and all the apparatus of a religious work, should be highly coloured in unrealistic blues, pinks, and purples. Of characteristic canvases by Velazquez, the one in which real atmosphere plays upon the widest range of colour is perhaps 'Las Hilanderas', otherwise 'The Spinners'.

VII

HIS MODELLING AND BRUSHWORK

WHILE speaking of colour one has gone some way towards describing the office of modelling; but there remains a little to say about this important subject. Modelling is the basis of the art of painting, the master-trick of the craft, since it is imposed upon the painter by the very convention which compels him to express depths of space and inclinations of surface by shades of colour laid on one plane. The shortest if not the best description of the convention of painting is given when you say that it compels you to have nothing to do with anything that cannot be shown at one view in a glass. This implies the single point of sight of perspective and the single focus of impressionism. In fact, the impressionists are the descendants of the perspectivists; they fight the same battle, and are pledged to the same cause, to show, not how things are, but how they seem. Notwithstanding the contrary opinion of certain painters, I cannot but consider modelling the most valuable acquirement of an impressionist, as with it he may render his impression of shape and yet neither rivet the eye nor detain the attention by defined lines or borders. It seems illogical, and it certainly violates the continuity of light to dispense with lines round large masses, while you carefully draw them with a rigger round eyes, mouths, noses, buttons, and other details. Brushwork then enters into the question, as it is the means used to carry out the logic of modelling, especially in the smaller sub-divisions of a picture where the minuter forms of detail must often be suggested by texture or a device of handling.

If one must divide the indivisible and name some quality of technique in which Velazquez most patently excelled, one feels inclined to choose his modelling. In expressing form by real light he finally attained to that Greek combination of broad, majestic beauty of effect, with the neatest perfection of finish. Other men, it will be said, have shown a fine command of form before him, and Velazquez himself could surely model well enough in his early works. The back of the blacksmith in 'The Forge of Vulcan' and the arm of Bacchus in 'The Topers', as well as the heads in that picture, are superb bits of modelling. In what consists the difference between this early rendering of form and the modelling of the later pictures? To some extent perhaps in a growing feeling for comparative strengths of definition, which enables him to avoid tricky or arbitrary expression, and to pass from piecemeal modelling to impressionistic modelling. A definition may not disappear in nature if you pry closely into it; but, when looked at together with a second one, firmer and yet soft in the ensemble, the first must often be made to disappear if due relative force is to be kept. A step in Velazquez's progress in comparative definition may be seen by comparing portraits of the second period, like the 'Sculptor Montañés', with close tight early work, such as 'Philip IV in Youth' (Prado), or even Philip, full length, in the National Gallery.[1] Though the pictures of the second

[1] The National Gallery 'Silver Philip' is also a work of the second period and, if the date 1636 is accepted for the Montañés portrait, almost contemporary with it. Both these pictures, however, may have been revised over a considerable period.

period are certainly freer, broader, and less hard than those of the first, perhaps they have lost something of the intimate rendering of form which was to be regained in final work, such as 'Philip IV in Old Age' (Prado) and 'Philip Old' (National Gallery).

Let us admit then that other men have felt form before Velazquez; it was his merit to have shown it under one effect of light and to have expressed it with the sorcery of truth and not by any kind of arbitrary modelling. The term needs explanation; I have used it for ten years, but the other day someone asked me if it meant the use of idealized forms instead of the actual shape of the model. Here, however, the term 'arbitrary' applies to the want of reality in the means used to express them, and not to any lack of actuality in the forms themselves. Idealized form can be rendered with the least possible convention, and with a fully coloured and real treatment of light, whereas actual form can be rendered with the much more conventional and unreal mediums of pure line or black and white monochrome. An extreme but well-known instance of arbitrary modelling may be seen in those maps which express the shape of a country by contour lines drawn at successive heights. The steeper the ground the closer the lines approach, till on a cliff they merge into a deep shade. If used as modelling, this arbitrary principle would assume a spectator in the zenith whose eye is the source of light, so that horizontal planes appear whitest and vertical ones darkest.

It is not necessary to describe all the kinds and degrees of arbitrariness in modelling which have been used both before and after Velazquez; a word or two must suffice. Leonardo da Vinci, when he was writing of modelling, blames the conventionality of previous practitioners as out of correspondence with the truths of real light. He accuses them of modelling by means of a monochromatic tint used in three or four bands of increasing darkness from full light to deep shadow. These gradation tints, something, by the way, like those used now in mechanical drawings, could be mixed with the local hue of a drapery or a flesh tint, or else might be superimposed in glazes. In both cases a sort of obligato accompaniment in monochrome was called upon to produce all the modifications of local colour that we understand by the word 'values'. Without doubt, succeeding painters have used more subtle methods of modelling, but whether they attain to the beauty and finesse of Raphael, of Rubens, of Titian, of Rembrandt, or only of Sir E. Burne-Jones, their modelling seems arbitrary and their beauties conventional beside the naturalism of Velazquez.

When we see a quite white world after a heavy fall of snow, we do not see a monochrome but the chromatic hues of a coloured atmospheric effect. Sometimes it is a tissue of rose, blue and yellow all in a high fairy-like key, or again it is a harmony of brown and silver; but, whatever it may be, it goes far to disprove the theory that a shadow is only a darker shade of a light. The shapes of this equally white ground are revealed by the various inclination of their slopes to the light, yet this light is yellow on one slope, blue on another, and by no means merely darker or brighter shades of one tint. The distances of the snow-fields are indicated by their absorption in atmospheric hues, but the foreground is not another shade of the colour that wraps the distance. A red, blue, or yellow world would also model chromatically under light, and so we may be sure that every change of plane in the real compositely-hued world should correspond in the picture to a change of value in true colour.

Velazquez's idea of finish in modelling consisted in making his rendering of light logical, convincing, and beautiful. He taught himself not to over-model every bit of a picture because he saw that the range of available values is graduated according to the inclination of real planes and not according to their size or structural importance. To burden a plane with smaller planes, perhaps steeper or equally steep, means frittering away the values that should not only distinguish, but eloquently proclaim important changes of surface. The constant repetition of sharp accidents tires the eye; it is like the false cry of wolf that forestalls the effect of the really momentous occasion. This appears especially evident in landscape, where it is counted unwise to pretend fully to outline and model objects too small properly to exhibit the effect of shadow and light. The artist who insists on giving such accidents an important treatment generally employs a false kind of definition which really belongs to the convention of outline drawing and not to that of full-toned oil painting. Indeed, the traditions of laborious or gorgeous styles of the past linger incongruously in later art, as buttons and lappets, the relics of former fashions, remain on the coats we wear to-day. In a difficult passage of naturalistic modelling, painters are apt to take refuge in the older conventions of line, which contradict and destroy the consistency and mystery of revelation by true light. If bad tone is often a relic of decorative or monochromatic styles, hard and linear definition often comes from traditions of primitive draughtsmanship.

In the art of outline drawing itself, it is held difficult to perceive the true sweep and sentiment of a long line which contains small indentations often steeper in their slopes than the main inclination of the large contour. In this case, however, experience proves that breadth of treatment can be cultivated by training. It is said that in France drawing can be taught even to a man without a turn for it, but, it may be added, drawing with no merit except that of a proportionate subordination of parts. However this may be, it is certainly more difficult to teach a man to perceive relative values of colour and relative forces of definition. He must not only learn to sweep his eye along one line, but to embrace a whole area with an imaginative grasp of sight. Hence it is easy to observe contiguous values and difficult to note the relation of value between tones separated from each other by a considerable angle at the observer's eye. It requires an impressionist to feel the connection between such values with anything like the sensation of certitude with which one feels the harmony of a chord. That is to say, it requires one whose faculty it is to conceive of all the spots and markings of a scene only in some relation to its whole aspect. The ensemble of a scene hypnotizes and fascinates an impressionist as if it were a real, personal, and indivisible entity and not a mere sum of small quantities.

Breadth of view was Velazquez's most admirable possession; by it he made composition, modelling, and style, the slaves of his impressions. This breadth of view led him in his later pictures to vary his manner of painting according to the sentiment of his impression, so that you will find in his work no pattern of brushwork, no settled degree of intimacy in the modelling, no constantly equal force of realization in edges, and, in short, no fixed habits or methods of expression. In the comparison of 'The Topers' with 'Las Meninas', it was pointed out that three single heads which are just sufficiently broad in treatment to look comfortable, would produce, if composed in one

I

frame, a pattern too crowded and spotty from a decorative point of view. But such a compilation of unmodified studies would sin also from an impressionistic point of view. It would imply three focuses of impression, and therefore whatever character each of the separate impressions might have possessed would be jostled out of existence by the others, and it would be impossible that there could be any agreement of meaning between the aspect of the picture and its technique.

To people who have never painted, such terms as impressions, fields of vision, and angles of sight, may seem fanciful, or at least irrelevant to art. An illustration may help to show them that there is no absolute realism of appearance, but that different eyes and different habits of looking at the world would manifest different qualities and different aspects of truth. When a man reads, he does not focus individual letters but takes in a whole line at a glance; so that in ordinary reading for pleasure he overlooks misspellings, reversed letters, etc. On the other hand, a child reading letter by letter, with a smaller field of impression, cannot avoid seeing such mistakes. The large print used for children is extremely fatiguing to grown people as in order to see at one time the amount of letters required to give them the current impression and meaning of writing, they have to work over an unusually wide field of sight. If they hold these large letters at a distance from the eye, proportionate to their size, they will observe that the eye defines differently, and altogether loses very fine strokes. It is easy to apply this to painting, and it may serve to show that what you look for you will see, let it be a large thing and a continuous meaning, or small things and a jerky interrupted meaning.

Many people must have noticed the occasional effect of

a portrait upon a blank canvas—an effect of grand importance, too often speedily impaired as the painter proceeds to fill in the space. This blank space happened to correspond roughly to the degree of attention which the painter had accorded to surroundings when he was painting the head; its emptiness justified the closeness of his modelling and the precision of his definitions. When he began to focus elsewhere and to fill in accessories, the head began to look mean and too tightly modelled. Velazquez's most closely-studied heads are for the most part isolated portraits, painted against utter blackness or against an atmospheric grey or fawn tone of great simplicity. Such are, for instance, 'The Crucifixion' (Prado, 1167), and 'Philip IV' (1182), in the same gallery. Indeed, the black blankness surrounding 'The Crucifixion' alone saves its antique Bellini-like details of lettering and wood-graining from looking commonplace and topographical. As he became an impressionist somewhat slowly, the qualities of modelling which Velazquez always possessed appear to best advantage in those early pictures which are simple busts, as 'Philip IV in Armour' and not those which are full-lengths, as 'Philip IV in Youth' or the older full-length of Philip in the National Gallery. In his later art, Velazquez never painted a wide view as he would a narrow one, nor a simple subject as a complicated one. When he painted a wide angle of sight, he either concentrated himself on a point, or steeped his whole canvas equally in a soft envelope of light. Indeed, whatever he painted, he always painted the quality of his attention to the scene, and, in virtue of that principle, his best pictures never look spotty, and never tempt one to cut them up into gem-like bits. His ensemble is always equally easy to grasp, whether he paints great groups like 'Las Meninas' and

'The Spinners', solitary full-lengths like 'Moenippus' and 'Æsop', costume-portraits like 'The Infanta Margarita', or simple busts like the head of Philip in old age.

But if the art of all these pictures is based on the same principles, and perhaps for that very reason, the technique is very different in them all. You may note a wonderful variety in Velazquez's style of modelling a head, not only in different periods of his life, but in pictures of the same period, and, what is more, in heads on the same canvas. Some heads are modelled very broadly and softly, without a sharp mark, a hard edge, or small steep planes. The surfaces slide into each other in a loose, supple manner, that almost makes them look as if they were shaped in jelly or fluid. Some consist of bold, rough-hewn planes which give a face the force and vigour of firm chiselling. Others, again, are completed to show the finest niceties of shape and inclination, with an intimacy of feeling and a delicacy of proportion that no man has ever equalled. The handling is always discreet and inspired by the necessities of the occasion; neither does it follow a determined pattern, which might impart a frozen and artificial look, nor does it seek an effect of *bravura* dexterity which might arrogate an undue share of attention and interest. Although no certain rule can be laid down, generally speaking, Velazquez inclines to brush in the obvious direction of the forms, so as to supplement tone and structure by the sentiment of the execution. In many cases, however, he smudges so subtly as to convey no sense of direct handling. The limb or object treated seems to grow mysteriously out of dusky depths and to be shaped by real light.

In the foregoing account of the art of Velazquez, it has been contended that his impulse to arrange a canvas grew out of the scene before his eyes; that his severe and stately colour is founded on nature, and that his execution becomes quiet and exact, or burly and impetuous, as the occasion demands. More than any other man's, his work convinces us that he knew what he saw and was incapable of self-deception; it is wholly free from haphazard passages, treacly approximations to tone, or clever tricks and processes that evade rather than resolve a difficulty. Above all, his art is interesting without the extravagance which may kindle a momentary excitement, but is apt, like a passionate mania for a woman, to die of satiety from its very violence. The restrained force and dignity of Velazquez inspire one with reverence and lasting respect; one cannot easily fathom the depth of his insight nor weary of his endless variety.

VIII

NOTES ON SOME OF HIS PICTURES

A FEW pictures may be mentioned as examples of his differences of treatment at various times of his life and in the service of various kinds of impression. 'Philip IV in Old Age' may be noted for the sweet finesse of the modelling, the lovely black of the clothes, and a command of colour in close ranges so supreme that the local tints of the flesh are preserved, and cannot anywhere be confounded with the soft iridescence of the luminous envelope. I scarcely noticed this canvas at first, but its unobtrusive thoroughness gained ground every day, and at last its silvery light fascinated me even more than the more striking illuminations of 'The Spinners', 'Æsop', or 'Moenippus'. It is smoother and more polished in surface than these pictures, making, indeed, quite a contrast to the particularly rough 'Æsop' near it; so that it has acquired a greener, mellower, and more varnished look, which adds to its appearance of extreme delicacy. One feels that this portrait of Philip goes beyond human powers in the intimacy of its modelling. It seems to challenge nature in finish, and one almost resents that art and nature should both triumph to this extent on the same canvas. Perhaps the more visionary modelling of the head in 'Moenippus', the grand unashamed *bravura* of 'Æsop', the looser, broader execution of the faces in 'Las

Meninas', 'The Spinners', and the 'Infanta Margarita', may be more impressively magisterial, because more artistic, or if you will, more artificial. The modelling of these pictures challenges less arrogantly the test of absolute truth. But it must be remembered that in the larger canvases the modelling is modified in style to suit different impressions and the convention of a wider view. This Philip in the Prado, like that in the National Gallery, only with less accessory, is a mere bust shown against simple gloom. Its extreme precision, and the close accuracy with which every refinement of plane and every delicacy of flesh tint is rendered are therefore justified, since the head, freed from distracting clamour of rival interests, alone occupies the eye and fixes the attention. It is possible to keep a tighter grip on the definitions, and, as it were, to screw the eye closer down to the forms than would be comfortable or natural in a wider or more complex subject.

Velazquez looks at a full-length or a portrait with accessories in quite a different mood. 'The Equestrian Philip' of his middle period he touches in summarily with fresh aerial colour squarely spread by large brush-strokes. The eye glances over the head taking in character as it would in the open air, without a too nice discrimination of varieties in flesh tint. 'Martínez Montañés' reminds one of a Carolus-Duran, with its bold planes as firm as if sculptured; while in 'The Infanta Margarita', on the other hand, the face looks soft and smooth owing to concealed flat modelling, and the head seems comparatively of small account, like that of a Greek statue. This quietude doubtless justifies itself by the exceeding brilliancy of the dress-painting, which captures so much of the attention.

The full lengths, 'Æsop' and 'Moenippus', differ no less from each other in workmanship than from the fore-going. 'Æsop', the most cleverly-handled of all Velaz-quez's heads, is the one that most supports the legend of his swaggering dexterity in flourishing a paintbrush. It is a rough impasto woven into a most marvellously expressive texture, which is unfortunately quite unreproducible in illustrations. 'Moenippus', again, is painted in large overlapping smears, very softly but very broadly, so that nothing specially arrests the eye, which floats over a face, figure, and accessories all bathed in liquid depths of air. In 'Las Meninas' you take in a populous area, you embrace a vast field of vision, a wide view, in fact, which demands and certainly receives the highest art of impressionistic treatment. Velazquez has centred the vision instead of spreading it equally over the field as Corot has done in many of his canvases. Yet this is contrived with so much art, that the careless might not recognize 'Las Meninas' as a work done on the same principle as some of those so-called eccentric pictures of recent impressionists.

Everyone will recall compositions in which a near figure, chair, table, or stretch of foreground, appears an enlarged and dislocated spectre, extravagantly membered of meaningless and accidental blotches. But these splashes obey a logical principle, although they may too often defeat their purpose by their infelicitous quaintness. The mind glides past these ghosts of objects unless they are made too strange; hence they should not fix the eye, but should play loosely in a free medium, and should carry with them no sharpness of definition, no small varieties of patch, no modelled detail. In comparison with other parts of the picture, they should have no attractive power over the eye, and yet they should come forward and stand in their right place. Now, after some study you will find in 'Las Meninas' this same art of distributing the attention. Wide as it is, one looks at it easily as a whole, and at every subdivision as an inseparable part of a scheme. The central Infanta, by the force of light, by the surrounding definitions, by the arrangement of the figures, by the strong opposition of the open door and by the character of the modelling, always holds the key of the situation. But this is not all, for the Dwarf closer to you on the right, as well as Velazquez farther off on the left, are by no means modelled in the same style as the Infanta. The Dwarf looks more diffused in definition and rather resembles the head of 'Moenippus' in its large looseness and its floating vagueness. This head, which is well to the side of the canvas, yet nearer to you than the Infanta, is worked with greater amplitude of modelling than the central figures, and with a less concentrated style and a more swimming touch. But there is no shocking distinction of brushwork in the picture, no perplexing splashes that detain a questioning mind even if they allow the eye to pass. At first sight all appears brushed with the same insidious naturalness of manner. Indeed, it is rather by subtlety of definition and the varying treatment of planes at their junctures, that the various interests of the picture are governed and subordinated. In the modern picture the trick is often too readily perceived and so appears unnatural. In 'Las Meninas' the eye is gratified unconsciously by this artifice and the impression of unity is made almost overwhelming, although the means used in no way intrude themselves, and you would swear that all was executed in the same style and by no subtler magic than a reflection in a mirror.

In the busier, richer, and more accentuated canvas of 'The Spinners', the shadowed left half acts as a foil to the right, and in its treatment we feel the master even more perhaps than in the lively right half which contains the heroic figure of the spinning girl. It is because this left half is complete and dignified yet not obtrusive that we admire the art with which it has been organized. True, it contains about as strong local colour as Velazquez ever painted, but the tints sleep in a rich, penumbra which serves to set off the highly-illuminated figure on the right. In this comparatively tranquil side of the picture, the spindle, the stool, the floor and the objects on it as well as the draped and shadowed figures, seem to quiver in a warm haze silvered with cool glints of light. Here Velazquez has reached the top point of telling suggestion, of choice touch, of nuanced softness, of comparative definition, and of courageous slashing force in the right place. But these two marvels do not quarrel; this rich circumambience of populous shadow and this dazzling creature emerging from shadowiness with the gesture of a goddess, set each other off and enhance each other's fascinations. Is not the magic of her exquisitely-turned head, and the magnificence of her sweeping gesture due, in part at least, to the natural mystery with which the stray curls, the shining arm, the modelled neck and body slide into the marvellous shadow in the angle of the room? The cool light, slightly greened now, which pervades 'The Spinners', comes to its culmination on this figure, and one should not overlook the painter's nice discrimination between the force of definitions in the passages from light to dark of the girl's chemise. The immense breadth of the surroundings, the fluid looseness of the inferior markings in 'The Spinners' helps to make the girl more really divine than the neighbouring Virgin by Murillo. In spite of her crescent moon, her cherubs, her pillowy clouds, and other religious paraphernalia, she is but a pretty ordinary girl whose hands, mouth, and hair are softly but cheaply modelled, in comparison to those of a figure by Velazquez.

In the octagon room close to 'The Spinners' hangs the costume-picture 'The Infanta Margarita'. She stands directly facing the light in a wonderfully elaborate balloon dress, embroidered with a complicated pattern of silver and pink and gleaming jewellery. In one hand she holds a rose, in the other a lace handkerchief, and on the left behind her in the shadow a red curtain droops in heavy folds. No pupil touched the smallest accessory of this extraordinary costume; lace, ruffles, embroidery, every inch of the dress is painted by Velazquez, with a running slippery touch which appears careless near at hand, but which at the focus gives colour, pattern, sparkle, and underlying form with the utmost precision and completeness. The shadow behind the figure is aerial in quality, deep but not heavy, and silvered like the passages in light, so that black would tell upon it as a rude brutality of tone. Near 'The Infanta Margarita', you may see work of many kinds; the beginnings of oil paint in a Van Eyck, contemporary art in the Murillo, and not far off A. Moro's 'Mary Tudor', painted for Philip II. Then there is 'Martin Ryckaert', Van Dyck's dark portrait of a man in a fur-lined robe, very finely and frankly painted, although without the finesse of the 'Infanta Margarita'. Rembrandt's 'Artemisia' may not rank among his good paintings, and certainly its gloom is heavy and its transitions from shadow to light are harsh in comparison to similar passages in the work of Velazquez. Examination of these pictures and others

will help to show the infinite delicacy which Velazquez
attained in the art of modelling, for beside his 'Infanta
Margarita' all other pictures seem to lack the subtlety of
real light.

It is instructive to compare the treatment of the dresses
in 'The Infanta Margarita' and in 'Las Meninas'. The
dress of the single portrait sparkles all over with vivacities
of touch, but the broad, flatter treatment of the dress in
the larger group better agrees with a rendering of attention spread over a wide view. Owing to this sensitive
feeling for the whole impression, 'Las Meninas', spread
out as it is and full of strong points, never tires the eye
and never appears uncomfortably crowded. Its detail
nowhere intrudes unduly and nowhere suggests a rival
impression to the main one. In fact, it is no more cut
up proportionately than the single portrait, although it
embraces many more figures. It was, however, this
dashing, rippling execution of 'The Infanta Margarita'
that chiefly struck the pupils of Velazquez, and one
can see very good imitations of it in the work of
his son-in-law, J. B. del Mazo.[1] Perhaps solider, sim-
pler work would have been more usefully studied.
Many painters in the present century have been taken
rather with the master's subordination of detail and his
breadth of modelling, than with his dexterity in brush
work.

In all the best canvases of Velazquez, you will find the
accessories vitalized by just degrees of force instead of
being killed by an equal realization all over the canvas.
So it is in the 'Moenippus', the 'Æsop', and the Dwarf

[1] A direct comparison is here possible, as Mazo, in 1664, executed a
copy of the Prado 'Infanta Margarita' which is now in Vienna. Mazo's
intervention in the Prado picture is limited to the head and curtain.

with a dog called 'Antonio el Inglés'.[1] The workmanship of this last a little resembles that of 'The Infanta Margarita' in its vivacious expression of detail with a flowing
brush. The ornaments of the dress, the hat and feather,
and the dog itself, are all given with a gusto that never
seems to interfere with true drawing and broad modelling. The handling of 'Æsop' is graver and more stately,
but everything here is also in its right place and of the right
force, down to the subdued finish and elegant accuracy of
the light on the water on the bucket. One cannot help
feeling that Manet, the painter of 'Le bon Bock', and other
magnificently painted heads, must have felt in close sympathy with the handling of the face in 'Æsop'. Again,
when one looks at the 'Sculptor Montañés', one thinks
of Carolus-Duran; of the Whistler of 'Lady Archibald
Campbell' when one sees 'Moenippus'; and of the
Sargent who painted 'Mrs. Hammersley' and 'El Jaleo',
when one stands before 'The Infanta Margarita' and 'The
Spinners'.[2]

In fact, when we look back upon the variety of all these
pictures, we are convinced that Velazquez never used style
for its own sake. Whether you look at a point of his
composition, colouring, modelling, or handling, it appears always to have been decided by the aspect of each
picture and not by preconceived principles. His composition is never a pattern forced upon nature, his drawing is
not an effort to realize abstract contours, his colour is not
the harmony of positive tints understood by a milliner,

[1] See note 1 on p. 95 above
[2] Sargent visited Madrid in the 1870s and made a series of copies of
Velazquez which today are highly valued when they reach the sale-room.
The series includes a head study and a small version of the equestrian
Balthasar Carlos: a head of 'Aesop'; the 'Bobo de Coria': The Infanta
Margarita: 'Las Meninas': and the central part of 'Las Hilanderas'.

his brush changes with his impressions, as the tones of a man's voice with his emotions.

Thus in 'Philip IV in Old Age' (Prado), no brushwork is visible as befits an almost perfect attempt at the illusion of light. This smoothness, however, has no kinship with the polish of Raphael, which was a mannerism applied to everything. The earlier 'Forge of Vulcan' shows a more evident workmanship, nowhere rough or sweeping, though you may note several instances of brushing across the shape of the limb, for Velazquez was never pedantic in his use of principles. 'The Spinners' may be quoted as an example of the painter's art of touching accessories broadly, and in this connection one should look also at the slashing lights on the horse in the 'Equestrian Olivares'. The 'Sculptor Montañés', the best portrait of the middle period, forestalls modern logicality of treatment; one may note the bold certainty with which Velazquez establishes the form of the eye socket, the planes of the nose and cheeks in this broad and stately portrait. No lines are wanted to bring out the shapes; the painter's science of values is all-sufficient. Even in 'The Infanta Margarita', which is a miracle of dexterous touch, the handling is obedient to fact and expresses matter before manner. The large, soft style of brushing used in 'Moenippus', 'Las Meninas', etc., may be seen on a smaller scale in the 'Philip IV Old' of the National Gallery. Lastly, the management of trees by Velazquez, in his later period, as in 'The Avenue' (Prado), may be compared in beauty, even to the work of Corot.[1] He has felt to the full the soft, bowery umbrageousness of trees, and has seen that for the most part they cut against the sky with a blurred,

[1] See note 1, p. 101 above. The 'Fountain of the Tritons', c. 1657, has a better claim to be an example of late Velazquez foliage.

vaporous line. As a tree is deep as well as broad, it can seldom relieve as a jagged line against a background; and as leaves are very small, and set one behind the other, the saw-edge of the contour of detachment becomes merely a line softened with such a burr as you see in drypoint.

IX

HIS RELATION TO OLDER ART

To the eye of the historian, Velazquez may seem to grow out of the main stem of art; he may appear to have his place in the orderly development of the history of painting. To the eye of the sympathetic modern painter, he seems an explosion of personality as disconnected with the art that immediately followed him as with that which preceded him. I believe that the expert in mannerisms has tried to fix his measuring apparatus upon the pictures of Velazquez, but to no good purpose. The counting of curls, the measuring of thumbs, the tracing of poses, may reveal something when applied to men who learnt to draw and paint formulas by rote, but must break down in the case of a man with whom drawing is not a habit but an art. Velazquez taught himself to picture the impression made by any sight upon his brain. This system of training, which aims at improving the sight, at cultivating a mood, at gaining a general faculty, has banished the other system of learning a set of proportions, a stock of patterns, a host of tips for drawing separate limbs and other natural objects. Nothing astonishes a modern painter more than to see a historian ransack every gallery to find a precedent for the style of a hand in a picture, rather than admit the possibility that an artist could choose one for himself in the vast magazine of nature. Personal preference, artistic impressionability, the counsel

of a passing mood, the testimony of a sensitive eye, are
not these sufficient reasons for the appearance of some
given form in a picture? Moreover, a picture cannot be
the efficient, the first cause of a picture; all true art ori-
ginates in the personal predilections of an individual mind,
and in personal sensitiveness to external nature. The rest
is disguised copying, artistic or inartistic mannerism. Now,
of all painters, Velazquez was the one who tampered least
with the integrity of his impression of the world. Every
one of his pictures was a fresh effort, less at finding a new
and striking subject than at realizing more absolutely a
way of seeing things in general that was personal to him.
Hence he never tired of repetition, for the good reason
that it was no repetition to him in the sense that successive
Madonnas and saints were to the early Italians, who
cooked them out of receipts for thumbs, hair, draperies,
ovals of faces, noses and poses.

This makes the study of his work at Madrid as trying
as the study of some dozen old Italian masters.

Although during a too short visit to the Prado I looked
at the rest of the gallery only as a background to the pictures of Velazquez, I cannot speak of him without feeling
a want of fuller knowledge and, above all, of the advantage of having made one or two copies. It was some con-
solation, after leaving Madrid, to hear from the Scottish
painter, Mr. John Lavery, that he had not found six
months of study and careful copying sufficient to settle
his opinions on the pictures of Velazquez.[1]   Upon his

[1] Sir John Lavery, R.A. (1856-1941), visited Madrid in 1891 and 1892,
and executed, among others, full-size copies of the Prado portraits of
Balthasar Carlos on horse-back, and of Queen Mariana. One of these
may well be the 'copy in Scotland' referred to by Stevenson. It may
be recalled that Lavery's well-known portrait of R. B. Cunninghame
Graham, now in the Glasgow Art Gallery, was painted in 1893 as a
homage to Velazquez.

K

return in a following year, he found unexpected beauties in some canvases, he looked at others as if he had never seen them before, while the copy that in Scotland had been to him and to other painters the very interpretation of Velazquez, now seemed lacking the essential spirit of the master. Thus, whether one gives a week or a year to the Prado, one comes back convinced that one cannot have sounded all the depths of a man who never did anything as a skilled automaton or a learned pedant.

Of course it is in the later canvases, in the works of the last dozen years of his life, that Velazquez makes the most marvellous use of paint. But the marvel is not of the kind one looks for. In the large impressionistic canvases of his later life, one might expect to see the bold, dexterous brusher surpassing even Ribera, Hals, or the mature Rembrandt in the *bravura* of his handiwork. On the contrary, as I have said, the paint at first sight scarcely appears to be intentionally handled; it seems put on, I might say, without art, if that did not give a false view; for in truth it is put on with consummate art in the interest of the whole canvas, and not for the style of the passage itself. Without flourish, for the most part without even an appearance of brush strokes, the paint is smeared in thin filmy scales which vary in size, looseness, and breadth, with the necessities of the subject and the composition. It is a style founded on the pursuit of more than usually just and subtle modelling, a modelling which changes character with the size of the canvas, with the width or narrowness of the field of view, and with the position near or far from the focus of impression of an object to be modelled. It is a style compatible with revision and correction, for it in no way depends upon the

integrity of some arbitrary pattern of touch, square, sweeping, or interwoven. This apparent artlessness surprises one
at first, but becomes in the end a chief charm of the later
Velazquez, who was too great, too earnest, too far-seeing,
to care for small affectations of manner. In these pictures
nothing seems to interpose between you and the mind of
Velazquez. You seem to be behind his eye, able to judge
and to feel, with all the power and sensitiveness of that
unrivalled organ. In a word, his work resembles the fine
writing in which style is so docile a servant of matter,
that it never draws attention to itself; you read as you
might eat a meal in the Arabian Nights, served by invisible hands.

In spite of the example of Velazquez, some modern
painters fear a close study of drawing, values, or modelling; and through their timidity they leave an impression
in a vague state, half-true, half-realized, a state of fever
or of sleepiness. Not nature, but the man's impression
of nature, should be complete and definite. Their fear
of drawing and modelling is unfounded; in the hands of
Velazquez these accomplishments never became mechanical, never degenerated from inspired seeing to trained
labour. Need we fear to advance towards truth and
accuracy, when he who adventured farthest seems to encourage us by the grandeur and surpassing sentiment that
rewarded his devotion to the *métier*?

Whilst looking at his pictures, one may remember
amongst his predecessors and the painters of his choice,
Caravaggio, Greco, Ribera, Sanchez Coello, and notably
Titian and Tintoretto. The spirit that animated Caravaggio and Ribera may be seen in the solidity, real form,
and fine handling of 'The Forge of Vulcan' and 'The
Topers'. In Greco you may see something of the

simplicity and sober colouring of his single portraits, and in Coello a prophecy of his flesh colours of grey ash quality and of his early accuracy in the accessories of dress.

Greco is often spoken of as a man to whom Velazquez was directly indebted for his style. While Greco certainly adopted a Spanish gravity of colouring, neither that nor his modelling was ever subtle or thoroughly natural. Yet in such portraits as Prado 810, 812, there is more supple-ness and breadth than Velazquez had ever displayed up to the date of Greco's death at Toledo.[1] One should compare these examples of Greco's work with the early 'Philip IV in Armour', and while one admits Greco's superior freedom and ease of style, one perhaps admires still more the inborn power of seeing shown by the model-ling of the mouth of the early Velazquez. While Velaz-quez ripened with age and practice, Greco was rather inclined to get rotten with facility.

Velazquez had opportunities of studying other painters than Greco as soon as he became Court painter, and it is known that his admiration was early turned to the work of Venice. He often praised Titian's execution as well as Tintoretto's rendering of light and the just depth of space. On the authority of Boschini, Carl Justi records a conver-sation between Salvator Rosa and Velazquez, which throws some light on the Spaniard's natural tastes. Salvator had asked whether after all he had seen in Italy he did not think Raphael the best, to which Velazquez replied, 'Raphael, to be plain with you, for I like to be candid and outspoken, does not please me at all.' Then Salvator said, 'In that case, there can apparently be nobody to your taste

[1] In making this comparison, Stevenson was incorrectly assuming that El Greco died in 1625, and not in 1614, when Velazquez was only fifteen years old.

in Italy, for to him we yield the crown.' And Velazquez answered, 'In Venice are found the good and the beautiful; to their brush I give the first place; it is Titian that bears the banner.' Velazquez, indeed, must have admired the breadth and envelopment of the pictures of Titian, Tintoretto, Correggio, Veronese, and certainly the style of such a portrait as the 'Andrea Odoni' by Lotto, which was exhibited in the New Gallery, January 1895.[1]   On the other hand, he could scarcely be expected to sympathize with the art of Raphael; and his outspokenness has been amply repaid in all ages by the frank dislike of all Raphaelites for his own work. We could not wish artists otherwise; were they tepid to the beauties they see in the world, they could arouse in us but a feeble response to their works. Art without personal prejudice would become an affair of science in which truth depends on argument and not on personal convictions. Painting, in that case, would be abandoned by artistic minds for some field of enterprise which was unattainable by mathematical processes, and which still offered free elbow-room for the sport of the emotions and the play of personality.

But before Velazquez saw Italy he must have seen the superb portrait 'Mary Tudor' (Prado, 2108), by Antonio Moro. The lesson of a picture which is absolutely sincere to the principle of sight of its author cannot have been lost upon Velazquez. This portrait stops everyone and communicates the shock of contact with a real person. I say 'shock' advisedly, for it is over-modelled after the manner of those who have fine eyes and are not impressionists. It betrays invincible perseverance, care, and close

---

[1] The portrait of Odoni by Lotto is at Hampton Court. Berenson's book on Lotto was originally published in 1895, the same year as the Venetian Exhibition referred to.

perception, but it reveals nothing magically like a late
portrait by Velazquez. Having seen it, you are done with
it, and cannot hope to find fresh beauties dawning on you
each time you return. The thing is too set, too tightly
frozen into definite lines in the features. Mary Tudor
would never have so looked to any one in her life. This
determined hunting down of every separate feature has
ended in something more rigid than flesh, something more
like a caricature than an impression, something more like
a diagram than the changeable reality of nature. It is a
record, perhaps, for the historian, not a revelation for the
poet. Yet beyond this ideal I scarcely think Velazquez
travelled until he was over thirty. The comparison of
the 'Mary Tudor' with the 'Sculptor Montañés', 'The
Spinners', and 'The Infanta Margarita', by Velazquez, is
worth making by anyone who goes to Madrid.

The power of seizing a speaking resemblance such as
we see in 'Mary Tudor' has been always accorded to
Velazquez. It is a merit which cannot be denied him as
it was denied Titian, Rembrandt, Rubens and other great
painters who often executed a fantasia on the *motif* of the
person painted. Titian's 'François Premier' is shrewdly
doubted on the score of likeness in the present day, and
Dutch burghers in the past preferred Van der Helst to
Rembrandt. It was in the cause of beauty that these great
artists sacrificed the accurate map of the features that
pleases family friends and the profusion of hard accessories
that ministers to family pride.

A painter may not with impunity take the free generous
style of Titian and Rembrandt and correct it with a dose
of the patient accuracy of tamer spirits. Grandeur and
carefulness will usually quarrel like a medicine of ill-mixed
ingredients in a patient's stomach. Men who have been

as conscientiously truthful as Velazquez have painted worse than he has and have not attained the same kind of truth. The intimacy which is so much admired in Velazquez was not arrived at by deliberate eclecticism, but by the inspiration of a genius for seeing things freshly. He learnt to see differently from Antonio Moro, to care for larger truths; and it was this fine imaginative seeing that gave a charm to the world in his eyes and prompted his brush to nobler fashions of expression. For what great thing can be done in art with only patience, method, and accuracy of eye? Those who have tried and failed, but who take heart to understand the success of great men, know that mere trouble only ends in elaboration of the part and disorganization of the whole; at best in the dull topographical chart of the features which misses the divine enchantment of the finest art. Yet one may search through the Prado in vain to find any portrait, outside of the work of Velazquez, more thoroughly studied than 'Mary Tudor', more evidently the report of a trustworthy eye. 'L'homme au gant', or the still finer 'Young Man unknown' by Titian in the Louvre, not to speak of 'Titian's Mistress', are incomparably more beautiful art than 'Mary Tudor'; they are less intimate, however. It is only Velazquez who is as penetrating as Moro, as poetical and artistic as Titian. 'Titian's Mistress', it is not possible to imagine even Velazquez able to better, but one feels that he, and perhaps he alone, could have corrected a certain hardness in the modelling of 'L'homme au gant', and an unwise precision in certain lines of the glove, hair, etc.

X

HIS INFLUENCE UPON RECENT ART

To see the Prado is to modify one's opinion of the novelty of recent art. Landscape and landscape with figure may be more independent of the past, but figure painting certainly owes much to Velazquez. Whether directly or indirectly, whether consciously or unconsciously, artists have decided after half a century of exploration to follow the path of Velazquez. Not that they have plagiarized, but that in the natural growth of ideas, the seed of thought has been blown from Spain to every part of the world. The process, however, was a slow one. Writers on Velazquez have been few; in the past Pacheco, the master and father-in-law of Velazquez, and Palomino, painter to Philip V; in the present century Sir W. Stirling-Maxwell, Richard Ford, T. Thoré, Carl Justi, and one or two others.[1] But writing can do nothing to help art, unless like a sign-post it makes painters aware of the road to a certain kind of art. They must walk it themselves, and we find that those who saw and spoke enthusiastically of Velazquez in the early portion of the century went little out of their way to understand him. Sir David Wilkie preferred 'The Topers' to the later work, and John Phillip, if he learnt anything from

[1] For other writers on Velazquez, and a summary of later researches, see the Appendix I and Appendix II.

Velazquez, learnt from the early pictures certain receipts in colouring and in handling a brush, but not the courage to work entirely without receipts.

The return to nature of the French Romantics of 1815 to 1855 was guided rather by the example of Rubens, Rembrandt, Lawrence, and Constable, than by that of Velazquez. A Gros, a Géricault, a Delacroix, however vigorously painted, shows only a realism of subject, of textures, of detail, of drawing, but never a realism of general aspect that could approach the convincing truth of the later impressionism of Velazquez. It was in landscape with figure that France independently worked out the principles of a new art, and even Corot seems to hold one hand to the Romantics, and the other to the schools of 1865-95. The names of Courbet, Manet, Carolus-Duran, Whistler, Henner, will occur to everyone as characteristic of the departure of the present movement in art. Without doubt, Bonnat, E. Delaunay, A. Legros, and others have revived our interest in style, our assiduity in modelling, but after fashions less particular to our own age.[1] I am more acquainted with M. Carolus-Duran's views and system than with those of others, and I think that he differs from French Romantics much as Velazquez differed from Rubens and Rembrandt.

Duran set himself to teach art less on the venerable principles of outline drawing than on a method adapted to his own fashion of looking at nature—by masses and by

[1] Stevenson's references to contemporary art reflect, of course, the tastes of his day, and names such as Henner, Bonnat, Delaunay, and Carolus-Duran are now less familiar than they were in the 1890s. Jacques Henner (1829-1905) was an Alsatian mythological and portrait painter much influenced by Correggio and the Venetians. Léon Bonnat (1833-1923), the founder of the Bonnat Museum at Bayonne, studied with Madrazo at Madrid and wrote the introduction to Beruete's *Velazquez*. Jules-Elie Delaunay (1828-91) was a historical and portrait painter born at Nantes.

constructive planes. Of course, Duran taught drawing, but
likely enough his method was not suitable to every kind
of talent, for he separated drawing from modelling with
the brush as little as possible. According to him the whole
art of expressing form should progress together and should
consist in expressing it, as we see it, by light. He regarded
drawing as the art of placing things rightly in depth as
well as in length and breadth; and for this purpose he
would call attention to various aspects of form—the inter-
section and prolongation of imaginary lines, the shape of
inclosed spaces, the interior contents of masses, the inclination of planes to light, and the expression or characteristic
tendency of any visible markings.

Very far back in history there was probably a sort of
folk-drawing as there was folk-music consisting of conventions for expressing individual objects to be learnt by
rote as we learn the shapes of the countries from an atlas.
Then came the stage of canons of proportion as we find
them still discussed by Dürer and Leonardo in their attempts to formalize the vague traditions of the past. From
this we pass in the books of that same Leonardo to the
third stage based on the sciences of perspective and anatomy. Relics of the first two stages are still to be found
amongst schoolboys who hand down 'tips' for drawing
men and objects, and never dream of going to look at
any object for themselves. 'Show me how to draw a
man', or 'I haven't learnt how one does a pig yet', are
phrases commonly heard amongst that kind of practi-
tioner. This rule of thumb tradition grows from various
sources, stray personal memories or observations, and fragmentary recollections of the work of such schools of first-
hand study from nature as the Greek and Assyrian. The
sciences in their turn were very useful to those who would

group figures from *chic*, cultivate improvement of type, and introduce tumbled and floating figures into great ceiling decorations.

As in Greece, so in later Europe, it was portraiture that kept art sincere and vital. But in spite of that influence, figure subjects remained long in the conventional stage. Leonardo's constant appeal to nature was not the mere commonplace saw that it is to-day. He found it necessary to enforce his view on every point; on drawing, on perspective, on chiaroscuro, on the value of colours at various distances, on the art of modelling, which he describes as too often consisting of an arbitrary passage from dark to light by the use of two or three stock tones brushed together.

Is it wonderful that you can apply Morelli's principles of criticism[1] to the Pre-Raphaelite Italian schools: that you can point to the thumbs, fingers, poses of the head, ovals of the face, and schemes of colour that the painters learnt by heart, and can even say from whom they learnt? The later Venetians broke away, and when you come to Velazquez, the system holds good as little as it can in our own day. Velazquez taught his eye so to report sight that he could render the familiar or the unfamiliar, and could communicate directly with what was before him without the intervention of traditional rules or scientific study. His name was for ever in the mouth of Carolus-Duran, when he spoke of the past, but it was not to induce his students to copy even Velazquez. For instance, the influence of Corot was great at that time, and I have heard Duran say, 'When you go into the fields you will not see a Corot;

[1] Giovanni Morelli (1816-91), Italian art historian and critic whose methods of attribution greatly influenced the young Bernard Berenson. The English translation of his *Italian Painters* appeared in 1892-93.

paint what you see.' He wished to direct their education
so that his pupils might attack nature from whatever side
they pleased. The prerogative of grasping what is before
you does not preclude you from afterwards learning to
do without the model, and to paint what you imagine
instead of what you see, but it provides you a perpetual
stronghold in case of defeat, and a base of operations for
future excursions into the unknown.

In his *Manual of Oil Painting* the Hon. John Collier[1]
says, 'To whatever use he may mean to put his art eventu-
ally, the one thing that he has to learn, *as a student*, is how
to represent faithfully any object that he has before him',
and in another place, 'there is nothing so deadening to
the imagination as to try to express it with inadequate
means'. Velazquez, by the admission of all the artists in
Rome, alone painted reality, the others, some decorative
convention. When, in the present century, truth of impression became the governing ideal of art, Velazquez
became the prophet of the new schools. At that time in
France, any *coterie* of young painters hired a studio, and
chose for themselves the master whose art promised them
guidance in a sympathetic path. Having themselves chosen
the direction, the students were all the more likely to bear
with the weariness and the obstacles of the road. For
those who had asked his aid, Carolus-Duran formulated
the principles of his own art, and enforced them by an
appeal to the practice of others and, before all, of Velazquez.

By his method of teaching, he hoped at least to give
the student a knowledge of what he saw, and a logical

[1] The Hon. John Collier, R.A. (1850-1934), well-known as a portrait
painter, was also an admirer and copyist of Velazquez. His *Manual of Oil
Painting* was published in 1886.

grasp of the principles of sight. After a slight search of proportions with charcoal, the places of masses were indicated with a rigger dipped in flowing pigment. No preparation in colour or monochrome was allowed, but the main planes of the face must be laid directly on the unprepared canvas with a broad brush. These few surfaces —three or four in the forehead, as many in the nose, and so forth—must be studied in shape and place, and particularly in the relative value of light that their various inclinations produce. They were painted quite broadly in even tones of flesh tint, and stood side by side like pieces of a mosaic, without fusion of their adjacent edges. No brushing of the edge of the hair into the face was permitted, no conventional bounding of eyes and features with lines that might deceive the student by their expression into the belief that false structure was truthful. In the next stage you were bound to proceed in the same manner by laying planes upon the junctions of the larger ones or by breaking the larger planes into smaller subordinate surfaces. You were never allowed to brush one surface into another, you must make a tone for each step of a gradation. Thus, you might never attempt to realize a tone or a passage by some hazardous uncontrollable process.

M. Carolus-Duran believed that if you do not approach tone by direct painting you will never know what you can do, and will never discover whether you really feel any given relation, or the values of any contrasting surfaces. The first stages of this work looked like portraits of wooden figures cut with a knife in sharp-edged, unsoftened facets. The effect on the Ruskinian of this hideous and pitiless logic was terrible. Most of them sickened at the strong medicine, and fled from the too heroic cure for the namby-pamby modelling which trusts for expression to a red line between the lips, a contour line to the nose, and a careful rigger track round the eyes and eyebrows. I have felt the first spasms of this disgust, and I praise the master who stayed, not the pupil who fled. If Duran was not squeamish at criticizing and touching these awful dolls, why should the pupil take pride in the weakness of his stomach? Duran had little patience with the aesthete and conventional sentimentalist, and nothing amused him more than the 'loss of my originality', a plea often put forward by men still blind to the ordinary aspect of nature. He was pitiless to the transparent colour dodge, the badger-hair hypocrisy, and the hopeful haphazard glazings of the sentimentalist who cannot shape a nose, and would show all Browning's works in a face.

This severe system, it must be remembered, served merely as the gymnastic of art, it was a means of education for the eye, not a trick of mannerism, or a ready-made style of painting. Had not Duran's studio been already described, I believe in the *Nineteenth Century*,[1] I should have said more of the teaching of a great painter whose only recognized master was Velazquez. There is, however, one point that I must mention, as it throws a light on the simplicity of Velazquez's flesh tints and the surprising subtlety and clearness of his modelling of shape. Everyone knows that insubordination of the eye or that false estimation of comparative importances in nature which led some painters to exaggerate spots of local colour, definitions of detail, reflected lights, or, in fact, anything dangerous to the peace of the ensemble. They

---

[1] It has proved impossible to trace any such detailed reference to Carolus-Duran in *The Nineteenth Century* between 1877 (the year of its foundation) and 1895 when Stevenson wrote.

so treated the skin, as to embarrass modelling, which is the first quality in a face, for the sake of accidental spots, which are of little count in that most even and luminous of substances, flesh.

If you will paint the trivial and the uncharacteristic, your picture must be commonplace; for what affects us in a picture is that for which it was painted, the things, in fact, for which the aspect of the canvas was designed. It is not sufficient to put things into a work of art, it is necessary to see that they look out from it perspicuously and with the greatest possible effect. A certain pattern, a certain shape, may be somewhere on a canvas, but it may lie there as well hid as the secret of a puzzle picture. The person who never sees anything particular to look at in a scene, alone thinks he can show everything to equal advantage by a labour of addition. The man with only a sense of decoration is saved this last humiliation of mistaking trouble for feeling, counting for being impressed, and measuring for seeing. He knows that every extra marking on a canvas increases the danger that a design may be choked and modelling buried in a welter of dots or a labyrinth of subordinate pattern. The English stipple of colours, chiefly seen about the eyes, ears, and the edges of shadows, always drew from Duran his famous 'Pourquoi ces trente-six mille couleurs.' We saw them, of course, not in nature, but in our memories of the cadmium, lake, green, and blue spots of the English pictures of that date. It was an easy task to seize on the excuse for these coloured spots, a difficult one to embrace the relations of the ensemble that reduced them to their true insignificance. The ornaments of an exaggerated colouring may be compared to the graces of rhyme in an accented language, such as English. Dignity stumbles over these recurrent obstacles, and if the sense skips them cleverly, it is at the expense of earnestness and reality.

The sight of Velazquez at Madrid does not make us look upon the works of Regnault, Courbet, Manet, Carolus-Duran, Monet, Henner, Whistler, Degas, Sargent and the rest, as plagiary. It rather gives the man of our century confidence that he is following a path not unlike that trod to such good purpose by the great Spaniard. To reach the goal of impressionism cost Velazquez thirty years of exploration, and then it was gained only for the expression of his own views. Velazquez, except in his few landscapes, never applied his principles to the thorough realization of *plein-air* effects. Thus, the path pursued by men of the present century, though by no means identical, passes through similar stages and progressions. Decorative formulas, and the successive realism of various separate qualities—subject, form, colour, and atmosphere—bestrew the path from Gros to Manet, just as they mark the stages in the development of the solitary Velazquez.

Corot and Millet took his principles into the open air; the first painting landscape with figures, the second figures with landscapes. Of these Corot was the purest impressionist, Millet hanging more evidently on the chain of Romantics from Michelangelo and Rembrandt to his own Barbizonian school. Regnault,[1] especially in the face of his 'Marshal Prim', shows a fellow-feeling with Velazquez in his second period of the great equestrian portraits. Duran avoided bright coloured subjects less than Velazquez, and reduced his handling to a more formal and logical pattern. Henner, half a Classic and half a Romantic

---

[1] Alexandre Georges Henri Regnault (1843-71), French portrait painter who was killed in the Franco-Prussian War. His equestrian portrait of Marshal Prim is in the Louvre. In 1868, on a visit to Madrid, he described Velazquez as 'the first painter in the world'.

by nature, took up the nude and worked it on more distinctly decorative *motifs* of colour, and on a softer but less
subtle principle of modelling.   Whistler combined a mor-
bid Japanese grace with the Spanish austerity of impression, and saw things with a *raffiné's* attraction to elegance,
and the quintessence of modishness.   In 'The Nocturnes',
in 'The Japaneseries', in 'Miss Alexander', in the portrait
of his mother, he breaks away into a game of his own.[1]
If not more original than others, Manet was perhaps the
strongest and widest in his originality of all the revivers
of impressionism.   He is as various in his moods as day-
light, and, except in one or two heads, such as 'Le Bon
Bock', shows nothing of his long study of Velazquez,
unless in the underlying convention common to all impressionists.

[1] Whistler, unlike Manet, never visited Madrid, but was greatly influenced by Velazquez and owned a number of photographs of his works.

L

XI

THE LESSON OF IMPRESSIONISM

THE more one sees of artists, the more one learns of their dependence on the model; the more one sees them eager to study the thing painted. But they apply to nature for different purposes, for anatomy, for surface character, for colour, for details, for movements, for values, for an impression of effect, for arrangements to fill a given space. Great painters of all schools from Leonardo to Whistler have so often acknowledged nature as the mistress that the admission becomes a truism were it not capable of being understood in so many different ways. It is a fresh reading of this precept that makes a new art; other considerations then become means to an end. Composition, colour, brushing, etc., receive a new consideration. Their effectiveness and their possibilities of style are overhauled and esteemed according as they can forward the expression of the central conception of natural beauty.

Carducho,[1] a colleague of Velazquez, waged war against the influence of naturalism in art, exalting traditional and learned painting above sensitiveness to nature. But Michelangelo, a fountain of learning and a head source

[1] The *Dialogos de Pintura* by Vicente Carducho were published in Madrid in 1633. Velazquez, of whom Carducho was jealous, is barely mentioned in this work.

of idealism, rose from the bowels of nature, springing, it is true, from another soil than Velazquez, from the objective rather than the subjective position. He grubbed into the depths of anatomy and studied nature as it was, concerning himself comparatively little with its aspect to the eye or its relation to the nerves of vision. To the learned decorator it seemed but a trivial thing to catch the flavour of life whilst filling a panel, to recreate in the subtle structures of the eye vibrations of a long hereditary past, and to recommend a present sentiment to the spectator's old habits of visual emotion. However, as we have seen in the history of mathematical invention, a new calculus is never to be counted useless. It is like the seeds which they say lie everywhere in the soil ready to sprout after fires or any favourable changes in the soil. So naturalism has grown like a grain of mustard-seed and the impressionism of Velazquez overshadows art. The test of a new thing is not utility, which may appear at any moment like a shoot with the first favouring breath of spring. The test is the kind and amount of human feeling and intellect put into the work. Could any fool do it? Now, in this matter of depicting truth there are eyesights of all grades of breadth, of grandeur, of subtlety, and art has more than the delicacy of a tripos examination in tailing out as in a foot-race all the talents and capabilities of the competitors.

The great idealist of Italy was admirable, but he is dead, his work is done, and when it was doing it was at least based on matter, on anatomy, on the laws of decoration. There is a modern idealist whose whole cause seems to be hatred of matter, of the truth, of the visible, of the real, and a consequent craving for the spiritual, the non-material. That this man should choose painting or sculpture, the most material, the most tied to representation of the arts seems indeed a non-sense.

Yet one cannot help feeling some sympathy with those who start on this hopeless cruise, who wreck the ship whilst steering to some visionary island of spiritualism. They are as those who dream of ideal love, and yet forgive no shortcoming, and persistently despise and misuse ordinary human affections, as those who wish for a perfect society and cannot take pains to understand their own day or their own country. This temperament is ruinous to the artist. He neglects the material base of art, despises drawing and modelling, and sacrifices the conquest of nature as readily as a faddist, the well-being of a great empire to his dreams. The true artist's thought is of his material, of its beauties, of its limitations, of its propriety to the task proposed. He has to achieve beauty, but under conditions—of fact, of decoration, of a medium. It may be seen in the work of Velazquez that there is no base reality; that the commonplace lies only in the method of a mean, a small, and an inartistic eye. It was not only his immediate subjects but the whole art of seeing that Velazquez dignified in his paintings.

Léon Pelouse,[1] the French landscape-painter, used to say that the gift of the naturalist lay in the power of recreating the eye of childhood. When the child first sees—before he can walk, before he can know what all these coloured spots of various shapes and strengths may mean —he receives from a field of sight an impression of the values of colour and the forces of definition utterly unadulterated by knowledge of distance, depth, shape, utility, and the commercial, religious, or sexual importance of

[1] Léon Pelouse (1838-91), French portrait and landscape painter active in Le Cernay, where Stevenson met him in 1879.

objects. Indeed, he is not biased by that chief disturber of impression, the knowledge that any objects exist; in fact, he sees men as trees walking. He sees patterns, and it takes him years to know what these patterns, these changing gradations, these varying smudges signify, and when he has learnt that, in proportion as he has succeeded, so he has ceased to know the original vision, and to perceive mentally the signs by which he originally determined the truth.

If the conventionality of an art that expresses three dimensions by two was not enough to assure us, then the foregoing statement must make it certain that the modern painter should concern himself very much about what seems, and scarcely at all about what is. Yet people will tell you that it is just the impressionist picture which looks strange to them, and the illogical dictionary of small objects which looks natural. The observation that a horse at a distance is not of the same shape as a horse near at hand is at least as old as Leonardo. He describes how the limbs disappear first, the neck and head next, as the distance increases, until you are aware only of an oblong or oval splash. But practice lagged long behind theory, and there are painters to-day, especially in England, who would not paint the real appearance of an object at different distances. They are behind the scenes, as it were, and, knowing that they are to produce a horse, they paint it exactly as they have studied it near at hand, only they make it small, like a toy, because it is far off. Some hundreds of years ago they would have refused even that concession to the then strange and novel art of perspective. These toy boats on the sea, these toy cows in the meadows, these toy soldiers in the battle-field, are not big things seen far off, but little miniatures near at hand, compelled by perspective to occupy a false position on the canvas.

Many Royal Academy pictures, and the most popular ones, are still full of these comic little dolls, which pretend to realism of effect. Such rude compilations of objects, studied at different focuses, are easily shown to be logically defective, but it is less easy to perceive the more subtle disaster incurred by a similar fault in figure subjects, where everything takes place somewhat close at hand. Comparison of the definitions and gradations of a fine Velazquez with those of an ordinary picture is, perhaps, the most ready way to perceive the vulgarity of the cheap method which exaggerates outlines, and replaces tone and gradation by false explanatory definition. To draw a silly line in a mouth, eye, or nose, where no line should be, merely because you have been taught painting by means of chalk-drawing, implies a gross violation of the lighting of a portrait, just as putting toy boats and cows in the distance implies a contradiction of perspective.

What is the harm, you may ask, of painting a picture piecemeal, since it is on the flat, and may be viewed from any distance? Cannot the canvas always be easily embraced by the eye as a whole? Quite so, and, because it then fails to give a truthful impression of the field it offers, it deceives expectation and violates the confidence of the eye. The compilation of sketches, or focuses of impression, induces false perspective, false values, false colour, a false proportion of detail to mass, and a combination of interests in false relation to the interests of the whole picture. Velazquez may have painted 'Las Meninas' how he pleased, yet he kept before himself a single impression of the scene, and therefore he succeeds in conveying it to the spectator. He may have studied each figure separately; he may have stood nearer to them in so doing than he makes the spectator appear to stand, but, if so, his artistic conviction of the true aspect of the ensemble was sufficiently strong to prevent him from executing his picture solely for the sake of each square yard he successively tackled. How many pictures of the scope of 'Las Meninas', or 'The Spinners', comfortably fill the eye as they do, and absorb the attention so justly and evenly all over that, at a certain distance, the sight neither wanders nor sticks at special points?

Everybody knows the condition under which a man receives an effective visual impression, one that goes to mould his view of the world. Whether he is looking at a piece of still life, or is standing in a vast landscape, he looks in a half dream; he ceases to think, to feel his own identity, for his whole consciousness is absorbed in the eye. At these moments a certain focus is used, a certain width of field is embraced, and these are not determined by the man's conscious will, but by the nature of his impression. To shift that focus to make that field larger or smaller is to destroy the mood which produced the impression.

If a cardboard of nearly ten inches wide be held at arm's-length it can be comfortably regarded as a whole, and of course any view, however distant, that it might cover. But if it be placed at forty feet from the eye, not without intentional effort or strain can the whole attention be exclusively centred upon its area. On the other hand, if it be held at about ten inches from the eye one can embrace as a whole no more than such a small bit of it as would cover the entire cardboard held at arm's-length. It would be wrong to say that it is impossible to

paint a larger field of sight than is naturally embraced as
one whole by the eye, but it is certain that one would
be compelled to determine the force of many values or
definitions in this too wide field by reason instead of by
feeling. Safety would lie only in a very conventional line
of treatment. Many realists, however, would paint the
scene covered by the cardboard held at ten inches from
the eye by adding together innumerable little impressions
of fields covered by the cardboard at forty feet from the
eye. As far as a perception of the ensemble goes, they
remain as much in the dark as a child of the final result
of a long sum in addition.

To lay down strict rules in such matters of feeling as
the width of an area of impression would be to fetter
practice, but it is curious to note that Leonardo, centuries
ago, suggested that the painter should be supposed to
stand at a distance from his picture of three times its
largest measurement. It was Leonardo also who proposed to show the effect of distance on local colour by
painting on a sheet of glass held up before the subject of
a picture. The value of the green of an elm at a hundred
yards from you could be thus compared with the value
of that same green at two or three hundred yards. In the
same way, if anyone desires to convince himself of the
subtleties of natural definitions, let him take a brush and
pretend to paint, on the pane of a window, the view
which he sees through the glass. When he would follow
the sinuosities of form, obey the subtle changes of definition, do justice to the myriad delicacies of detail, he will
confess that he has undertaken a task too delicate for the
nicest of Pre-Raphaelite nigglers. It will be plain to him
that the scene must be 'treated', and the main relations
alone given. Twigs, stones, slates, grass, leaves, can only

be suggested; an attempt to define them really could result in nothing but a coarse travesty, which must inevitably lessen the effect of the more important markings. By varying his distance from the pane, the experimenter may convince himself that the difficulties of painting the scene increase as the field of sight widens. He will see that a wide angle must be treated differently from a narrow one, a *motif* with one bold, detaching mass, differently from one containing several smaller importances. Besides meeting these more evident exigencies, he must allow something for personal feeling. He will find out how to realize on canvas the impression of some object, how it should be placed on the canvas, how much field shall surround it, and what portion of that field, if any, represents a space lightly skimmed by the mind, but a space nevertheless necessary to impart some quality or some meaning to the chief object.

It may be argued that you have only to imagine a glass subtending to the eye, the same angle as the said pane of glass, but much farther off, and a brush fifty yards long to solve the difficulties of landscape painting. Only in life-size painting of figure or still life can this be realized practically, and then only mechanical difficulties are removed. The problems of how to employ modelling, relative forces of definition, and range of colour, in treating scenes of various widths, depths, and fulness of interest, still remain to be solved by artistic feeling. But in this life-size painting the task is more evident, at least to the reason, and for this cause, possibly, impressionism was first fully made manifest in the work of a portrait painter, Velazquez.

People who use both the terms, realism and impressionism, discriminate their meanings, and certainly those who paint impressionistically will not confound their practice with that of some realists. But many people, in speaking of impressionism, imply that it must be unmodelled, scarce drawn, roughly surfaced, ugly, at least commonplace in subject. Others hold that whatever else it may do, it must represent, like an instantaneous photograph, passing movements by blotches and blurs, and show you strange and really unimpressionistic attitudes never seen in life, but mechanically revealed by the camera. The work of Velazquez should be sufficient evidence to persuade them that they misunderstand the question.

Let us look at some of the uses of the term realism. After an age dealing with saints in the clouds, or gods in Olympus, a man may be called a realist because he paints real life, a battle, the coronation of an emperor, or boors drinking. This distinction of subject has been shown on an earlier page to have little weight in the art of painting; and one may observe that, after courtly subjects are exhausted, this bastard realism of *motif* is confined to low life. Nevertheless, there is a realism, not literary, but pictorial; the realism of treatment which is applicable to any subject, religious, mythological, heroic, courtly, or low-lived, even to still life and landscape. Orpheus, Endymion, Hope, Love, Caesar crossing the Rubicon, or a man digging potatoes, may any of them be conceived realistically, and painted from the model. But when we admit this, and discriminate realism of subject from realism of treatment, we still meet with various degrees of realism. This man may be realistic in form only, and fanciful in lighting and relations of value. That man, again, may idealize form and yet paint it under a realistic effect. In fact, realism of treatment depends on a piecemeal sort of observation which may be taken in

instalments by successive schools. There is a realism of
drawing, of effect, of local colour, of atmosphere, of
values and all and any of these are pictorial in their
nature.

Now, impressionism allows many and divers impressions, but each records a truth of general aspect. The
whole effect of the canvas conveys a definite idea which
has ordered every element—drawing, colour, and definition. Schools of painters are not, of course, divided absolutely into decorative, realist and impressionist; but we
name them after the prevailing intention of their works.
The difference between realism and impressionism may
be illustrated out of the past by the contrast between the
Eclectics and the Naturalists on the one hand, and Velazquez on the other. The art of the first added, the other
sprouted fresh qualities; one held its virtues in solution,
the other in chemical combination.

Those who have not been taught from the beginning in
an impressionistic school must remember difficulties which
beset them when they were working from nature, and
will recall how they only slowly began to appreciate the
meaning and the necessity of working from a single impression. How often it seemed to them impossible to
finish a picture. The more closely they applied themselves to study and complete a part, the more it seemed to
change to their eyes, and to invalidate their previous observations. After having left his canvas for a rest such a
man came back to find this or that edge cut as if with a
knife, this shadow which should be blue and broad, hot
and speckled, and certainly all the mystery, grandeur,
or delicacy of the natural model painted out in commonplace. Again and again he tries, and each time that he
brings a fresh eye to bear upon the model, he finds

that all its characteristic beauty has evaporated from his work. He may never attempt to enter upon completeness, he is kept in the ante-room of preliminary changes.

Now, all his separate observations may have been true, but they were all made under different conditions of attention to the scene; whereas, until every part of the picture has been observed in subservience to the impression of the whole, completeness can never be even begun. The largeness, the dignity, the swim of nature seen under a distributed attention is continually contradicted by the appearances which result from separate observations made upon smaller fields of sight. A shadow on the yellow sand will alternately seem cold or warm, blue or orange, according to the concentration or diffusion of the sight. Everyone knows that when a shadow is looked at alone it appears more full of colours than when the surrounding sunlit parts of the view are taken in and are allowed to operate on the shadow.

Many people must have seen English painters who went out of their way to confuse their eyesight and destroy all unity of impression. Some begin a large landscape at the top of one corner, and finish it all the way down bit by bit. Others make use of all kinds of dodges to deceive themselves as to the impression a natural scene has made on their senses. These make a tunnel with their hands to shut out everything but the one patch of colour they are matching. These hold up white paper to gauge a value; these match tints upon a palette-knife held against the hues of nature; these cut holes in a card to look through; and these peep through their legs, their half-shut eyes, or into a small black mirror. Such devices confound and obliterate the natural impression when they are used as a means of finishing a picture. Yet they have some of them a true use, which is to persuade a beginner of the relativity of tones and definitions, and their dependence upon general impressions. Surely, however, it cannot but lead to painting false aspects if one should try to learn anything spectacular from nature seen under such conditions. I have often seen men painting sunsets who would shade out the sky with a hat or hand that they might see what they were pleased to call the true colour of the ground. Of course, the grass instantly became of quite another colour to what it had been when the sky entered the painter's eyes at the same time. But they seemed unaware that they were painting by this process two quite different effects in one frame.

English teaching has been contrary to impressionism, and Velazquez has not been sufficiently, or at any rate rightly, admired. Many painters and writers of influence have condemned impressionism in a manner which showed that they neither knew nor cared anything about it. Whatever has been gained in England in this direction lately has been gained at the bayonet point of abuse and strong language. The English schools never taught one to 'place' a figure or cast on the canvas. They would not permit of blocking in either squarely or roundly. They expected you to begin a thing by finishing. They accustomed the student from the outset of his career to overlook subtle differences of large planes, to miss the broader sweep of a line for the sake of tight detailed modelling, and the exaggerated indenting of small bays in an outline. They gave gold medals to chalk drawings in which every little muscle was modelled up to a high light, whilst an important change of plane, such as the set-back of the chest, was shown by a wrong general value. It is not wonderful that people so taught saw only one side of the art of Velazquez, and that their system of teaching is now abandoned for one which has been, to a large extent, based on the practice of the great Spanish impressionist.

APPENDIX I

VELAZQUEZ RESEARCH SINCE
STEVENSON (1900-1960)

Looking back from the tercentenary year of Velazquez's death, sixty-five years after Stevenson's book was first published, it is now somewhat difficult to imagine that only within about twice that span of time—the last hundred and thirty years—has appreciation in Britain of the genius of this great artist developed from almost total ignorance, to its present peak of universal acknowledgment and scholarly appraisal. The systematic study in this country of Velazquez and of Spanish art (as opposed to the fragmentary accounts and lists of pictures compiled by early writers such as Cumberland, Buchanan, and Ford) can be said to date from the days when first the Peninsular War, and later such key mid-century art dispersals as the Meade, Standish, and Louis-Philippe sales, released to discriminating British collectors the majority of the great Spanish pictures still in Britain to-day. At the same time as these sales, by a happy coincidence, there was published a pioneer contribution to our knowledge of Spanish painting and especially of Velazquez which, like Stevenson's later contribution in the field of aesthetic criticism, now tends to be somewhat overlooked. Sir William Stirling-Maxwell's *Annals of the Artists of Spain*, which appeared in 1848, when the author was only thirty, is by any standards

a considerable feat of erudition for so young a man, and
the chapters on Velazquez, published separately in 1855,
and in French, with a revised catalogue by W. Burger in
1865, are still to-day outstanding for their accuracy. A
second edition of the *Annals*, incorporating the author's
own revisions, was published posthumously in 1891: Stirling himself had died in 1878, but it is not too much to
say that the achievements of the immediately following
twenty years—the classical age of Velazquez scholarship
which produced in rapid succession the works of Curtis,
Cruzada Villaamil, Justi, Stevenson, and Beruete—owe
much to his inspiration.

An examination of these works, and of the later catalogues compiled during the first half of the twentieth century, gives the measure of how art-historical scholarship
has, over the years, sifted and resifted the work of Velazquez and gradually has eliminated the many items, which,
in earlier days, passed under his name in sale-room catalogues and collections: for example, Stirling, in 1848, in
the first *catalogue raisonné* of Velazquez to be drawn up
in this or indeed in any country, listed no fewer than 219
works as autograph, of which 76 were in Britain. Cruzada
Villaamil (1885) also included over 200 works, as did Dr.
G. C. Williamson when, in 1899, he added a catalogue
to the second edition of Stevenson. If we exclude Curtis
(1883) and Mayer (1936),[1] whose broadly based catalogues
of nearly 600 items sought to include every known picture
having Velazquez relationships, the list since Stevenson's

[1] It is not widely known that Mayer published in Paris in 1940 (anonymously owing to the German occupation) a last small book on Velazquez
in which he drew up a basic catalogue of a hundred works, including
several very speculative ones not mentioned by any previous critics. This
book also incorporates his revised views on the chronology of some of
the pictures, but it has not been closely followed in the later Spanish
catalogues.

day has been greatly curtailed: Beruete (1906) reduced it to only 92 autograph works; Allende-Salazar (1925) to 114; Lafuente Ferrari (1943-44) and Gaya Nuño (1953) to about 130; and Pantorba (1955) to 117, of which 17 were in Britain. It seems possible, however, that this depurative process has by now reached its limit, and that some additions to the definitive list, rather than deletions, may occur from time to time as new documentary or stylistic evidence accumulates. Indeed, during the last ten years in this country alone, three Velazquez portraits have been either discovered or newly documented to a degree which has demanded their reappraisal as autograph works; these are the Bankes portrait of Cardinal Camillo Massimi, painted by Velazquez in Rome in 1650; the 'Huth' or Louis-Philippe full-length portrait of Queen Isabella of Bourbon, listed and valued as a Velazquez in the Spanish Royal Collections and now known to have been adapted from an earlier portrait which lies beneath it; and, finally, the bust portrait of Archbishop Fernando de Valdés in the Bainbrigge Collection, to which, on the evidence of old complete copies, the signed Velazquez hand fragment in the Royal Palace at Madrid may once have belonged.[1] Other outstanding Velazquez paintings established since 1900 include the Frick portrait of Philip IV at Fraga; the so-called Villahermosa group of portraits of Philip IV, Olivares, Diego del Corral and his wife; the Beit and Chicago versions of the Mulatto Servant; the Prado portrait of Sor Jerónima de la Fuente; and the Detroit portrait of an unknown man; while several others, previously recorded but insufficiently studied, have been admitted to

[1] For details of these three paintings see respectively *Burlington Magazine*, August 1958, pp. 279-80; *Connoisseur*, May 1958, pp. 238-44; *Connoisseur*, March 1960, pp. 102-4; and *Varia Velazqueña*, Vol. I (1960), pp. 310-15.

M

the definitive catalogues by the slow process of exhaustive analysis.

Closely allied to documentary research has been what might be termed the 'humanistic' approach to Velazquez studies—the definition of the personality of the artist by an examination of his setting, beliefs, and way of life. Pioneered by Justi in his classic work, Spanish writers such as Sánchez Cantón, Ortega y Gasset, and Lafuente Ferrari have made some notable contributions in this field (such as the analysis of Velazquez's library and personal possessions) which have shed much new light on his mental and stylistic development, and in particular on the sources which prompted his approximation of mythology to everyday life in such pictures as 'Los Borrachos' and 'Las Hilanderas'.

The establishment of a Velazquez chronology by means of documentary evidence has also been actively pursued since Stevenson's day, first by Mayer and Von Loga and later by Spanish scholars such as Allende-Salazar, to whom are due the first attempts at systematization on these lines. Since about 1940, however, commencing with Mayer's last work and the catalogues of Lafuente Ferrari, there has been a definite reaction in favour of a reassessment of this chronology on purely stylistic evidence—a critical method which it will have been seen that Stevenson, as early as 1895, was already pursuing. The division of Velazquez's output into three periods punctuated by the two Italian visits of 1629-31 and 1649-50, can now be accepted as definitive on historical and documentary grounds, but the formerly rather rigidly applied theory of a stylistic progression from realism to impressionism is giving way to the realization, backed by scientific evidence, that Velazquez not only constantly revised works which remained accessible to him, sometimes over a considerable period,

but also could adopt at will a tighter or freer style according to his mood and the exigencies of his subject. This
fact, well emphasized by Stevenson in his chapter on
Velazquez's modelling and brushwork, and coupled with
new documentary evidence in a few cases (e.g. the dates
of the Court Dwarfs), has led to a more even allocation
over the period between the two Italian visits (1630-50)
of a number of works which earlier writers had regarded
as very late. There is still, however, a considerable measure of disagreement in the literature on dating, and it is
here, perhaps, that the development of Velazquez as a
colourist could be given more attention than it has yet
received, for an artist's use of colour is less susceptible
than the rest of his technique to apparent displacements
in time. One regrets that Stevenson, in his excellent
chapter on Velazquez's colour, did not enlarge on this
aspect as an aid to chronology.

Another remarkable gap in modern Velazquez studies
is that despite the many monographs and specialist works
on the master, his studio and school, and the number and
precise identification of his pupils and assistants, remain
almost as uninvestigated as they were in Stevenson's time.
This point has been well emphasized by Dr. Halldor
Soehner in an interesting survey of past and present trends
in Velazquez research, published in Madrid in 1951. Re-
ferring to Mayer's 1936 catalogue, he points out that
'while on the one hand there are a great number of pictures, and on the other there have come down to us a
series of names of artists close to Velazquez, no correla-
tion has been achieved, despite great effort, between the
pictures and the names. The studio work of the master
remains in the shadows.' A list of the recorded pupils
of Velazquez, or of those known to have collaborated

with him, confirms this view, for mostly they are little more than 'names' that might be virtually unknown to us but for a brief mention by Palomino, Ceán Bermúdez, or other early chroniclers.[1] There is, however, one notable exception: a monograph on Juan Bautista Martínez del Mazo seems long overdue, and it is, indeed, the measure of the uncertainties still surrounding the school of Velazquez that the relative contributions of Velazquez and his son-in-law even to such an important picture as the 'View of Saragossa' in the Prado should still be under discussion. As a portrait as well as a landscape painter, del Mazo deserves to be taken out from the shadow of his father-in-law and established with a much more identifiable personality of his own; this should be fully possible in his case though not, perhaps, in that of Juan de Pareja, the other principal assistant, or in that of the elusive Antonio Puga, to whom a number of Velazquez school genre pictures might be attributed, if more was known about him. Meanwhile one can only agree with Gaya Nuño that 'the more one investigates the personality and work of Velazquez, the more he stands alone, and the emptier are his immediate surroundings'.

Greater attention has been paid since 1900 to Velazquez's compositional methods and to the analysis of his forms, but general acceptance of Beruete's view that he was as uninfluenced by his predecessors as he was isolated from his contemporaries, discouraged for a long time any speculation as to possible models for his works. In 1947, however, Angulo Iñiguez, in an analysis of eleven of Velazquez's principal paintings, was able to demonstrate

[1] Apart from Mazo, Pareja, and Puga, the following is a list of the principal recorded pupils or collaborators of Velazquez: T. de Aguiar; A. Alfaro y Gamez; B. M. de Aguero; F. de Burgos Mantilla; M. de la Cruz; J. de la Corte; A. Deleito; D. de Lucena; F. Palacios; B. Román; N. de Villacis.

substantial borrowings from Veronese, El Greco, Michelangelo, Salamón, Dürer, and Titian, while the Caravagesque and Flemish origins of the early *bodegón* paintings have been similarly explored by Soehner and others. This has led to some modification of the view propounded by Justi that Velazquez was first and foremost an impressionist whose later pictures are, like snapshots, a selection by the eye of a single visual field, whereas they are actually very carefully contrived compositions which brilliantly unify several such fields. Stevenson's early grasp of this fundamental point is evident if one compares his discussions of 'Las Meninas' and 'Las Hilanderas', with many contemporary and even much later criticisms of these pictures which emphasize only their casual, almost accidental, origins.

To-day, it is the 'modernity' of Velazquez which constitutes one of his greatest appeals and is one of the chief subjects of contemporary criticism: the only difference is that we now prefer to see him not, like Stevenson, as an 'explosion of personality', but in the context of the new 'modern' attitude of mind which, as Professor Maravall has demonstrated in a recent study, gradually permeated the whole life of the century in which he lived. The influence of Velazquez on British and Continental nineteenth-century artists is one of the principal themes of this book and need not be stressed again here, but it is also very apparent from the copies or free interpretations of his works, which have been produced in such numbers from the days of early Victorian academicians such as 'Spanish' Phillip, through the whole range of the Whistlerian and French impressionists to Picasso.[1] These, in themselves,

[1] To mention only a few documented examples, Velazquez has been copied since the time of Goya by Phillip, Carolus-Duran, Regnault, Manet, Whistler, Sargent, Fantin-Latour, Lavery, Furse, and Collier. Picasso's famous variations on 'Las Meninas' are, of course, in a class apart.

would provide fascinating material for a further incursion into the world of Stevenson and his contemporaries.

In this brief summary of the present state of Velazquez researches, it has been possible only to mention those aspects of it which have seemed particularly relevant to Stevenson's essay: for instance, Velazquez's Sevillian origins and his relations with his Spanish fellow-artists Murillo, Cano, Tristán, and Zurbarán, are barely touched upon by Stevenson and are, indeed, in some ways as unexplored as the problem of his studio and imitators; so, as has been briefly noted, is the question of his influence, if any, on certain foreign contemporaries such as Gerard Terborch and Louis Le Nain. The Tercentenary Year has, however, produced a large *corpus* of literature of varying merit and significance which, selected and classified in the bibliography, may provide some additional specialist aid to the appreciation of what a writer in the *Edinburgh Review* (January 1901) described as 'Stevenson's suggestive book, which will stimulate students for a long time to come'—particularly, it is hoped, now that it is again accessible in this new edition.

T. C.

APPENDIX II

SELECT BIBLIOGRAPHY

This short classified bibliography contains the principal standard works on Velazquez and also certain articles on the more specialized aspects of Velazquez criticism discussed by Stevenson. For an exhaustive bibliography of Velazquez the reader should refer to the works of Trapier and Pantorba listed below.

HISTORICAL SOURCES

Carducho, Vicente. *Dialogos de la pintura.* Madrid 1633.

Pacheco, Francisco. *Arte de la Pintura; su antiguedad y grandezas.* Seville 1649.

Palomino de Castro y Velasco, Antonio. *El Museo Pictórico y Escala óptica,* Vol. II. Madrid 1724. (An English summary of this volume was published in London in 1739.)

Ponz, Antonio. *Viaje de España,* Vol. VI. Madrid 1776.

Cumberland, Richard. *Anecdotes of Eminent Painters in Spain.* London 1787.

Ceán Bermúdez, Juan Agustín. *Diccionario Histórico de los mas ilustres Profesores de las Bellas Artes en España.* Madrid 1800. (With Supplement by Conde de la Viñaza, Madrid 1894.)

Varia Velazqueña, Vol. II. Ministerio de Educación Nacional, Madrid 1960. (Contains useful transcripts of all early texts, commentaries, and documents which refer to Velazquez, including those listed above.)

MONOGRAPHS AND CATALOGUES

Stirling-Maxwell, Sir William. *Annals of the Artists of Spain.* 3 vols. London 1848. Revised Edition, 4 vols. London 1891.

—— *Velazquez and his Works.* London 1855. French translation, with a catalogue by W. Burger (T. Thoré). Paris 1865.

Curtis, Charles B. *Velazquez and Murillo. A Descriptive and Historical Catalogue.* London and New York 1883.

Cruzada Villaamil, Gregorio. *Anales de la vida y de las obras de Diego Velazquez.* Madrid 1885.

Justi, Carl. *Diego Velazquez und sein Jahrhundert.* Bonn 1888. (English translation *Diego Velazquez and His Times*, London 1889.) Second revised German edition, Bonn 1903, 1921, and Zurich 1933 (the last with a catalogue by Ludwig Goldscheider). Spanish edition, with an Appendix and catalogue by J. A. Gaya Nuño, Madrid 1953.

Lefort, Paul. *Velazquez.* Paris 1888.

Armstrong, Sir Walter. *Velazquez, a Study of his Life and Art.* London 1896.

Beruete, Aureliano de. *Velazquez.* Paris 1898. English translation, London 1906.

Calvert, A. F. and Hartley, G. C. *Velazquez, an Account of his Life and Works.* London 1908.

Mayer, August L. *Velazquez.* Berlin 1924.

Allende-Salazar, Juan A. *Velazquez. Klassiker der Kunst.* Stuttgart 1925. (Catalogue, with text by Walter Gensel.)

Mayer, August L. *Velazquez, a Catalogue Raisonné of the Paintings and Drawings.* London 1936.

—— *Velazquez.* Paris 1940. (Published anonymously.)

Lafuente Ferrari, Enrique. *Velazquez.* London 1943. Idem. Switzerland (Skira) 1960.

—— *Velazquez.* Barcelona 1944.

Trapier, Elizabeth du Gué. *Velazquez.* New York 1948.

Pantorba, Bernardino de. *La Vida y la Obra de Velazquez.* Madrid 1955.

Gerstenberg, Kurt. *Velazquez.* Munich 1957.

Velazquez y lo Velazqueño. Catalogue of the Tercentenary Exhibition. Madrid 1960. (Compiled by Valentín de Sambricio.)

López-Rey, José. *Velazquez. A Catalogue Raisonné of his Œuvre, with an Introductory Study, Velazquez's Work and World.* (To be published in London in 1962.)

DOCUMENTARY AND GENERAL RESEARCH

Zarco del Valle, M. R. *Documentos inéditos para la historia de las Bellas Artes en España*, Vol. 55. Madrid 1870.

Madrazo, Pedro de. *Viaje artístico de tres siglos por las colecciones de cuadros de los Reyes de España.* Barcelona 1884.

Mesonero Romanos, Manuel. *Velazquez fuera del Museo del Prado.* Madrid 1899.

Tormo, Elías. 'Velazquez; el Salón de Reinos del Buen Retiro y el poeta del Palacio y del pintor'. *Boletín de la Sociedad Española de Excursiones*, 1911-12.

Sánchez Cantón, F. J. *La librería de Velazquez*. Madrid 1925.

—— *Como vivía Velazquez*. *Archivo Español de Arte*. Madrid 1942.

Moreno Villa, José. *Locos, enanos, negros y niños palaciegos*. Mexico 1939.

Ortega y Gasset, José. *Velazquez*. Madrid 1959.

Soehner, Halldor. *El estado actual de la investigación sobre Velazquez*. Clavileño, Madrid, May-June 1951.

Varia Velazqueña, Vol. I. Madrid 1960. (Numerous general articles.)

THE PRADO MUSEUM

Madrazo, Pedro de. *Catálogo descriptivo e histórico del Museo del Prado*. Madrid 1872. (The so-called 'catálogo extenso' of which only the first volume containing the Italian and Spanish Schools was published.)

Ricketts, C. S. *The Prado and its Masterpieces*. London 1903.

Beroqui, Pedro. *El Museo del Prado (Notas para su historia)*. Madrid 1930-32.

Sánchez Cantón, F. J. *Guide to the Prado Museum*. Madrid 1959.

—— *The Prado*. London 1959.

INDIVIDUAL WORKS DISCUSSED BY STEVENSON

Sentenach, N. 'Las Lanzas y Las Hilanderas'. *Boletín de la Sociedad Española de Excursiones*, May 1894.

Beruete, Aureliano de. 'La Venus del Espejo'. *Cultura Española*. Madrid 1906.

Beruete y Moret, Aureliano de. 'Velazquez ou Mazo? Les portraits de Pulido Pareja'. *Gazette des Beaux-Arts*, April-June 1917.

Justi, Ludwig. 'Die landschaften des Velazquez'. Berlin, *Repertorium für Kunstwissenschaft*, 1927.

Sánchez Cantón, F. J. *Las Meninas y sus personajes*. Barcelona 1943.

Angulo Iñiguez, Diego. 'Las Hilanderas'. *Archivo Español de Arte*, January-March 1948.

Tolnay, C. de. 'Las Hilanderas y Las Meninas'. *Gazette des Beaux Arts*, January 1949. 'Las pinturas mitológicas de Velazquez'. *Archivo Español de Arte*, January-March 1961.

Lozoya, Marqués de. *La rendición de Breda*. Barcelona 1953.

Sánchez Cantón, F. J. 'La Venus del Espejo'. *Archivo Español de Arte*, April-September 1960. 'Sobre el "Martínez Montañés" de Velazquez'. *Archivo Español de Arte*, January-March 1961.

Diez del Corral, Luis. 'Los paisajes de la Villa de Medicis y el espiritu de la antiguedad'. *Varia Velazqueña*, Vol. I. Madrid 1960.

Angulo Iñiguez, Diego. 'Fábulas mitológicas de Velazquez'. *Goya,* Madrid, July-October 1960.

Pantorba, Bernardino de. 'Notas sobre cuadros de Velazquez perdidos'. *Varia Velazqueña,* Vol. I. Madrid 1960.

López-Rey, J. 'A Pseudo Velazquez: the Picture of a Dwarf with a Dog'. *Gazette des Beaux-Arts,* October-December 1950.

TEACHERS AND PRECURSORS

Robinson, Sir J. C. 'The Bodegones and Early Works of Velazquez'. *Burlington Magazine* 1906-7.

Rodriguez Marín, Francisco. *Francisco Pacheco, maestro de Velazquez.* Madrid 1923.

Sentenach, N. *The Painters of the School of Seville.* London 1911.

Soehner, H. 'Die Herkunft der Bodegones Velazquez'. *Varia Velazqueña,* Vol. I. Madrid 1960.

PUPILS AND FOLLOWERS

Beruete y Moret, Aureliano de. *The School of Madrid.* London 1909.

Gaya Nuño, J. A. 'Juan Bautista del Mazo, el gran discípulo de Velazquez'. *Varia Velazqueña,* Vol. I. Madrid 1960.

Hernández Perera, J. 'Carreño y Velazquez'. *Varia Velazqueña,* Vol. I. Madrid 1960.

Pijoán, José. 'Terborch y Velazquez'. *Goya,* Madrid, November-December 1954.

Lorente, Manuel. 'La Vista de Zaragoza por Velazquez y Mazo'. *Archivo Español de Arte,* April-September 1960.

Temboury Alvarez, Juan. 'Alonso Cano y Velazquez'. *Varia Velazqueña,* Vol. I. Madrid 1960.

COMPOSITION

Angulo Iñiguez, Diego. *Velazquez. Como compuso sus principales cuadros.* Seville 1947.

Camón Aznar, José. 'El concepto del espacio en Velazquez'. *Varia Velazqueña,* Vol. I. Madrid 1960.

COLOUR, BRUSHWORK, AND MODELLING

Beruete y Moret, Aureliano de. *La Paleta de Velazquez.* Madrid 1921.

López-Rey, José. 'Pincelada y Imagen en Velazquez'. *Varia Velazqueña,* Vol. I. Madrid 1960.

VELAZQUEZ IN ITALY

Harris, Enriqueta. 'La Misión de Velazquez en Italia'. *Archivo Español de Arte*, April–September 1960.

Lorente, Manuel. 'Velazquez y La Villa Medicis'. *Varia Velazqueña*, Vol. I. Madrid 1960.

VELAZQUEZ AND MODERN ART

Camón Aznar, José. 'El impresionismo en Velazquez'. *Goya*, July–October 1960.

Guinard, Paul. 'Velazquez et les Romantiques francais'. *Varia Velazqueña*, Vol. I. Madrid 1960.

Benet, Rafael. 'Manet y Renoir ante Velazquez'. *Varia Velazqueña*, Vol. I. Madrid 1960.

Lambert, Elie. 'Velazquez y Manet'. *Goya*, Madrid, July–October 1960.

Maravall, José Antonio. *Velazquez y el espíritu de la modernidad*. Madrid 1960.

Gallego, Julián. 'Velazquez and Modern Art'. UNESCO *Courier*, December 1960.

INDEX